SOLO

SOLO

The Great Adventures Alone

Edited by
HARRY ROSKOLENKO

Ρ⅄Ρ

A PLAYBOY PRESS BOOK

Published simultaneously in the United States and Canada by Playboy Press, Chicago, Illinois. Printed in the United States of America. Library of Congress Catalog Card Number: 73–84658. First edition.

PLAYBOY and Rabbit Head design are trademarks of Playboy, 919 North Michigan Avenue, Chicago, Illinois 60611 (U.S.A.), Reg. U.S. Pat. Off., marca registrada, marque déposée.

ACKNOWLEDGMENTS

Excerpt from *"Gipsy Moth* Circles the World" by Sir Francis Chichester. Reprinted by permission of Coward McCann & Geohegan, Inc. from *Gipsy Moth Circles the World* by Sir Francis Chichester. Copyright © 1967 by Sir Francis Chichester.

"The Bombard Story" by Alain Bombard. From *Great True Tales of Human Endurance* by Pamela Search. Published by Arco Publications Ltd. Reprinted by permission.

Excerpt from "Whom the Sea Has Taken" by William Willis. Published by Meredith Press, New York, 1966. Reprinted by permission of Paul R. Reynolds, Inc., New York.

"Soviet Captain Reports Evidence of Willis Death," Moscow, September 30, 1968. Reprinted from The Associated Press by permission.

"Alone Against the Arctic" by Colin Irwin. Reprinted from *True* Magazine, March 1972. Copyright © Colin Irwin, 1972.

"First Power Flight at Kitty Hawk" by Fred C. Kelly. From *The Wright Brothers* by Fred C. Kelly, published by Farrar, Straus & Giroux, Inc., 1951. Reprinted by permission of the Estate of Fred C. Kelly.

"Lindbergh's Own Story" by Charles A. Lindbergh. Copyright © 1927 by The New York Times Company. Reprinted by permission.

"Across the Atlantic—Solo" by Amelia Earhart. From *The Fun of It* by Amelia Earhart. Published by Brewer, Warren & Putnam, 1932. Reprinted by permission of Harcourt, Brace, Jovanovich, Inc.

"Navy Declassifies Its Files on Amelia Earhart." Originally published July 13, 1967. Reprinted by permission of United Press International.

Excerpt from "Alone" by Richard E. Byrd. Reprinted by permission of G. P. Putnam's Sons from *Alone* by Richard E. Byrd. Copyright 1938 by Richard E. Byrd, renewed © 1966 by Marie A. Byrd.

"Half-Way Round the World on Horseback" by Aimé Felix Tschiffely. Originally published as *Tschiffely's Ride*, Simon & Schuster, 1933. Reprinted from *Tales of Hazard*, ed. by H.C. Armstrong. John Lane, The Bodley Head; 1932.

CONTENTS

8   THE MOUNTAINS

INTRODUCTION

Man, from his very beginning, became the explorer and the adventurer in the normal process of developing his early history. He crawled, walked, climbed, swam, rode. By the time he reached the 20th Century, he flew in a plane.

Through prehistoric times, every long journey was an act of discovery. Wandering, searching for food and comfort, he was always on the verge of new frontiers and new illuminations as he traveled unknown seas and oceans to new lands. During the Age of the Vikings, a thousand years ago, North America was discovered, as well as the world of the primitive Indian. Every long sea voyage enlarged his vision of nature, mystery, science —and man.

Thor Heyerdahl, in our time, in his Pacific Ocean voyage on his raft, the *Kon-Tiki,* proved it possible that Polynesian civilization was related to North and South America. Yet man, always the inventor and discoverer, was often man going off alone, and the uniqueness of his desire to go SOLO may reflect the fact that aspects of civilization were even then crowding in on him. His epic wanderings made him the temporary master of oceans, mountains, skies, and in the process he could also rediscover his own self.

Why does man persist in pitting himself against these endless challenges? Why does he long to adventure, to discover, to climb? Mallory's classic reply to the question of why he climbed Mt. Everest gives us part of the answer: "Because," he said, "*it was there.*" When the sky finally became a highway for crossing the oceans and the continents, and aviators finally circled the world, the moon was the next irresistible challenge . . . and a new era was upon us.

This anthology, varied in its solo adventuring, reaches out in the language of the men who did what they did. What could the lonely sea voyager discover in himself as he crossed oceans on a raft or a small boat? Was it always some private need for heroism? Did it also contain an element of altruism? After all, the North and the South Poles, when conquered, gave mankind greater mastery of the once-impassable areas of the frozen world. When Wilbur Wright finally flew in a nameless plane at Kitty Hawk on December 17, 1903, the world changed all of its cosmic values. Man, airborne, soon became man rocket-borne —and once again fantasy became reality.

Whatever the human and spiritual reasons for the amazing journeys in this anthology of courageously gifted people, we have only their universal explanation: They did it because they had to—and they had to do it alone.

The history of exploration and great adventuring is a succession of extraordinary undertakings by great captains and their teams. This book, however, does not dwell on the essence of team traveling. It is confined to those men who chose to seek and meet adventure and challenge by themselves, pitting themselves against themselves and nature, the human quest to go, to see, to climb, to sail, to fly beyond the beyond—alone. The author, J.R.L. Anderson, calls it *The Ulysses Factor.* It is, of course, intellectually understood to be totally dangerous, and yet man will act it out again and again. Indeed, the eccentric, the loner, the solo adventurer acts out not only his own but other people's dreams.

The men in this book are men of our time. Some of them were

no longer in their prime, like the yachtsman Sir Francis Chichester and the 71-year-old raftsman William Willis. The sea has taken both of them in its fashion. There is the mystic, Maurice Wilson, the only mountain climber to attempt Mt. Everest alone. His failure was as grandiose as were the reasons why he climbed and died on that austere mountain. And Alain Bombard, the young French doctor who sailed in a rubber boat for 65 days, living off the sea to test the capacity of a shipwrecked sailor to exist on plankton and seawater. He could, because Bombard did.

In this anthology there are scientists, hermits, mystics, mariners—the heroic private breed. They are poets in the acting-it-out processes, and men of amazing self-reliance. It is the ego exploring the exoticism within one's self and the limitations of the self. We may not have a Homer in this collection, but all the men in this book are natural writers, and to read them is to glow with the inner and outer achievements of their solo adventuring. A horseman (Tschiffely) traveled 10,000 miles in two years en route from the pampas of the Argentine to Washington, D.C. He is now a legend. Tazieff, a scientist-writer and the most noted of volcanologists, writes with wonderful colors about the trembling earth at the crater of Kituro, always ready to blow its bubbling top. Tom Neale and Sylvan Hart, both of them eccentrics, became hermits, one of them on an atoll in the South Pacific, and the other in the wilderness of Idaho. They write as latter-day Thoreaus living off the good earth and more than happy to be there alone.

There is Admiral Richard E. Byrd, aviator and polar explorer, spending the long Antarctic winter alone—to test his own resources against himself and frozen nature—and the epochal flights of Charles Lindbergh and Amelia Earhart, the solo hoppers of an era when planes were hardly the astonishing and sturdy machines they are today. It was their singular will and ability that made them masters of their flights, to become airborne into history. And there is the young Englishman, Colin

Irwin, attempting the brutalizing transit of the Northwest Passage in 1971 in a 19-foot enclosed boat, a feat that took Amundsen three years and three men in a large boat to accomplish in 1906.

This is man sailing, flying, climbing and riding in the areas and nature of his own choosing, soloing in great adventures alone. And as Tennyson wrote about *Ulysses*:

We are not now that strength which in old days
Moved earth and heaven, that which we are, we are—
One equal temper of heroic hearts,
Made weak by time and fate, but strong in will
To strive, to seek, to find, and not to yield.

1

THE SEA

GIPSY MOTH CIRCLES THE WORLD

Sir Francis Chichester

"The only way to live life to the full is to do something that depends on both the brain and on physical sense and action," wrote Francis Chichester. The son of a North Devon country minister, he became a well-to-do map publisher after working at various jobs in New Zealand, including lumberjacking, gold prospecting and boxing. Returning to England in 1929, he got his flying license—and started for Australia in a single-engine airplane named *Gipsy Moth*, covering 12,600 miles in 180 hours.

In 1930 he was to make the longest seaplane voyage, covering 1,450 miles in a single flight. In 1931 he set out again in a seaplane, this time hoping to circle the world. Starting from Sydney, he reached Japan, crashed and was invalided for five years. When he recovered in 1936 he made a solo flight from Sydney to London. Always sickly, and a practicing vegetarian, he took up yachting and established several world records in transatlantic solo racing.

On August 23, 1966, he left Plymouth, England, in *Gipsy Moth IV* on his world-circling clipper-route voyage.

I crossed the line as the gun fired and was off on my 14,000-mile sail. It was a sparkling, sunny morning and I added my big staysail and the mizzen as I made my way out of Plymouth Sound. Eight-eight minutes after the start, Eddystone Lighthouse was abeam, and I had been making good 7¾ knots. I turned in for a short sleep, and immediately got a dollop of sea on to my shoulder in the bunk from one of the ventilators. I cursed it heartily. . . .

At 07.00 there was a rough sea with a 24- to 32-knot wind, and I still had only the mizzen and jib set. I had no appetite, but had been actually sick only once. By noon I had made good 190 miles in the first 25 hours of the voyage. I got a sextant fix from the sun, and finished hoisting the mainsail and the staysail genoa by 13.30. I found that the windward tiller line from the self-steering gear had stranded. This was the start of almost endless trouble with making the boat self-steer, though mercifully I did not then know it. These troubles were not the fault of the self-steering gear; the load on the rudder was so great that a tremendous strain was imposed on the tiller lines connecting the self-steering gear to the tiller. . . .

I could still eat nothing, but at noon on August 29 I managed to get down a little food—my first meal since leaving Plymouth two days before. It had been a bad morning. I was having great difficulty in handling the self-steering gear, and the boat. A 35-knot squall from the northwest had set *Gipsy Moth* griping up to windward, overpowering the self-steering gear. I dropped the 300-foot jib and, after a rest, hoisted the 200-foot working jib. . . .

I had sailed 556 miles in the first four days, and a spell of bright sunshine made me feel better. I went on with my housekeeping, hanging out clothes to dry, and tackled various deck-jobs, working in shorts only, which was very pleasant. I sent the kedge anchor down, and secured it in the forecabin. This made the foredeck much clearer for working. I had had a big nylon net specially made which I had fitted on the deck amidships for stowing bagged-up sails, and now I rigged an extra line over the top of this net for security in bad weather. . . .

By the night of August 31, I was clear of the main steamer

lanes, which was a relief, though I was still near the route marked from the Channel to Recife, in Brazil. I reckoned that this was not an overcrowded route. I was past the latitude of Cape Finisterre in northwest Spain, and hoped for a northerly airstream. . . .

I picked up the aero beacon at Funchal, Madeira, and got a bearing on it, which agreed with the plotted position. At 01.40 on September 5, I was 77 miles from Porto Santo. It was a lovely moonlit night. The swell had eased, and the dark surface of the sea was sprinkled with gleaming white horses. In the morning, when I was breakfasting in the cockpit, I saw my first flying fish.

At 11.00 that morning I could see Porto Santo dead ahead, faint but unmistakable. I prepared a hoist of my number, GAKK, allotted to me as the nearest thing possible to the registration letters of my Gipsy Moth plane in 1929, GAAKK. By lunchtime the island of Porto Santo was abeam. *Gipsy Moth* was galloping downwind in bright sunlight and a brisk breeze, sailing at 7.8 knots. . . .

Every day was getting hotter. On September 8, I logged: "I have to be careful to cover up before going out under the high sun; I take everything off as soon as I am below." The day's run was only 96 miles and of that 17½ miles was due to the Canary Current, which is an extension of the Gulf Stream, branching off round the Azores, and flowing south-south-westwards past the Canary Isles. . . .

On September 11, I sailed into the tropics, and had a good day's run of 194 miles, the best so far of the passage. It was very hot, 82° in the shade, and later, in the dark, it was awe-inspiring on the foredeck when doing 10 knots; it gave the impression of a runaway horse. The white water rushing past was shot with brilliant dots of phosphorescence. But it was difficult to sleep with the rough riding. Two hours after midnight (September 12) I was again worrying about *Gipsy Moth*'s tendency to broach to. . . .

September 17 brought my 65th birthday. I had a big time

with a fresh-water wash, followed by opening Sheila's birthday present, a luxurious and most practical suit of silk pyjamas. I shed a tear to think of her kindness and love, and all the happiness we have had together since 1937. I started celebrating my birthday by drinking a bottle of wine given me by Monica Cooper and other members of our map-making firm for a birthday present. . . .

In the evening I set the mainsail in place of the trysail for the South-East Trade Wind. It was a lovely evening, and lovely sailing. *Gipsy Moth* was now on the wind doing 5½ knots, and headed south by west. It was now that I experienced one of the big setbacks of the voyage.

Let me explain the situation. From where I was then at 4° N and 21° W the old Clipper Way curved slightly westward down through the South Atlantic to Ilha da Trinidade from where the curve changed gently to the southeast, passing close to Tristan da Cunha Island to reach the Greenwich Meridian at 40° S. The distance along this route from where I was to where the Clipper Way passed south of the Cape of Good Hope was roughly 5,000 miles or 7.14 knots for 700 hours. The first 1,500 miles of this Clipper Way passed through the South-East Trade Wind belt. Southeast was the direction of the Cape so both the clippers and *Gipsy Moth* would be hard on the wind for at least the first 1,500 miles. I had felt quite sure that this was one point of sailing in which *Gipsy Moth* would excel, and I had checked that she would sail nearly as close to the wind as a Twelve Meter in a 30-knot wind in the comparatively smooth water of the Solent. I had based my plans for a 100-day attempt on sailing much closer to the wind in this belt than the clippers could have done. In other words I had planned to cut the corner and save no less than 800 miles on the way down to the Cape. . . .

On September 23 I lunched off my first crop of cress grown on the premises, and very good it was, too, with Barmene, some mayonnaise, a little garlic and some raisins. I was determined to grow some more cress, but was worried by the appalling lethargy which seemed to swamp me. Anything that required remembering and doing twice daily (watering cress, for instance) seemed a burden. It was hot, too hot to stay on deck long during the heat of the day, and pretty hot below—83° at 5 P.M. . . .

On my 32nd day out (September 28) I was 1,940 miles from where I should cross the Greenwich Meridian at 40° S. *Cutty Sark*, on her 32nd day, was 1,900 miles from where she crossed the meridian. So I figured that the *Cutty Sark* was only some 40 miles ahead of me after 32 days. The weather grew much colder, and I began wearing woolen shirts and trousers below deck. I felt that the Antarctic was creeping up! . . .

On October 1, five weeks out, I began to feel hungry again, and had a wonderful breakfast. I had slept well, and woke feeling properly rested. I went on deck and changed up the storm jib to the working jib. This gave me an appetite, and I found a flying fish on deck, provided for my breakfast. I cleaned and cooked the fish, and that breakfast stays in my memory. The menu was:

1 grapefruit (about one-quarter thrown away because of
    going bad)
2 potatoes fried up with the flying fish
2 slices of wholemeal toast with butter and marmalade
1½ mugs of coffee. . . .

On the night of October 2 I saw the Southern Cross for the first time since 1938, when I was coming home with Sheila from New Zealand. That was a thrill, though in the meantime one of the four stars of the Cross had become faint, which marred the handsome constellation.

Working up my sights at noon on October 18 I found that I was well over halfway to Australia—at noon that day I had sailed 7,300 miles, and had 6,570 miles to go to Sydney Heads. As if to celebrate this achievement the day changed like magic from grey with misty low clouds and overcast to a bright blue clear sky, with a darker, but still bright, blue sea. . . .

It was damnably uncomfortable. The wind went up to 55

knots, and the yacht was thrown about in all directions. Water kept forcing its way under the cabin hatch whenever a wave hit the deck. My sextant, which I stowed for safety in a cabin berth —fortunately in its box—was thrown out onto the cabin floor. I had one wave come right over me when I was in the cockpit; the water felt oddly warm, and the wave did not seem to strike with much force, I suppose because we were not moving. The air was biting cold with hail. . . .

The boom came over with an almighty "wham," the vang tearing a stanchion out of the deck. As it came across, the main-sheet slide shot across the track rail, and tore out the permanent stop screwed to the end of the rail. The slide holding two parts of the mainsheet came off the rail or horse. . . .

OVERCOMING DISASTER

I began to understand why these lonely seas are called "The Roaring Forties." It is the noise of the wind in the rigging. I would not call it a roar exactly, but I know of no other way of describing it—a hard, compelling noise that seems unique to those latitudes. In the days of the clippers, with their forests of masts and rigging, the noise must have been awe-inspiring.

My sense of spiritual loneliness continued. This Southern Indian Ocean was like no sea I had met before. It is difficult to paint the picture with words of what it was like down in the Southern Ocean in those spring months. I have sailed across the North Atlantic six times, three times alone, and experienced winds up to 100 miles per hour (87 knots) there, but looking back it seemed so safe compared with this Southern Ocean stuff. . . .

But I was improving all the time, and on November 24 I logged:

"Still driving hard through grey-green seas, and grey sky of low overcast. The rig seems to be spoiling me, keeping course at 7 to 7½ knots all through the night, except for periodic roarings in the rigging and bashings of waves over the deck when a wave throws the boat's head off to the northeast or even further to the north; but each time so far, after rough going for a few minutes, the steering sail has brought her back on course. It is 9½ hours since I touched tiller or rope. Long may it continue; it smacks of the marvelous to me!". . .

On November 29 I had sailed for 14 days since the self-steering bust, and had made good 1,808 miles, an average of 120 miles per day. This was good going because, quite apart from my self-steering difficulties, I was missing one of my best driving sails. Alas, it was not good enough to reach Sydney in the 100 days. I still had 1,057 miles to go and only six days of the 100 left. . . .

With daybreak of the 5th [December] the wind fell light and also backed, thereby heading me worse than ever. On that day my hundredth day ran out. I reported:

"In the last four days I have made good only 279 miles, plugging into a head-on easterly, mostly of gale force. It was equivalent to beating up the English Channel for four days against a gale for a third of the time, and a Force 4 wind for the rest. Twice I had to heave to when the boat was being pounded too hard by the seas. It was thick dirty weather, and I did not get a positive position check until I reached Cape Liptrap at noon today.". . .

On the morning of the 10th, *Gipsy Moth* was becalmed, but in the afternoon a breeze came in from the northeast. I was headed again, but it was a fine sparkling day. I called up Sydney Radio and asked them to give Sheila a message that I had been becalmed since midnight, had only just begun to sail again, and had 102 miles to go. . . .

However, I plugged along, sailing as hard as I could. At least it was a lovely day. At 10.00 in the morning I tacked off Cape

Baily at the southern headland of Botany Bay. I had only 13½ miles to go to Sydney Heads. A smart blue police launch put out from Botany Bay, spoke to me, and gave me a welcome. I hoisted the White Ensign and the RYS burgee. Slowly I beat up the coast. As the land heated up, a sea breeze caused the wind to veer in direction, and I could nearly lay a course for Sydney, having to tack off-shore only for a mile or two every 5 miles. . . .

   Gipsy Moth entered Sydney Heads at 4.30 P.M. on December 12 thus taking 107 days 5½ hours by the calendar or to be exact 106 days 20½ hours actual time after allowing for the change of longitude. The distance sailed was 14,100 miles. This was the total of the point to point noon to noon daily runs. . . .

Seven weeks later, after a reunion with his wife and son, who had flown out from England, and essential repairs made to the Gipsy Moth, *Chichester set out on the second leg of his solo circumnavigation of the world. In Sydney he was warned by the famous yachtsman and square-rigger skipper Alan Villiers not to go on. Said Captain Villiers: "I beg Chichester not to attempt it. The outward trip he made is simple compared with this one. That yacht may suddenly be lifted on boiling seas and rushed headlong towards the Horn."*

   In the Sunday Express *on January 1, 1967, an interview with an English clairvoyant brought out more dire warnings: "Lone yachtsman Francis Chichester is doomed to failure in his attempt to sail around the world. This is the opinion of clairvoyant Marjorie Staves. 'But he will come home to one of the greatest welcomes in our history,' she told me. 'He will give up due to lack of physical strength. But any man who has such great mental strength as to make me feel it across thousands of miles is going to make a wonderful try.' "*

   At last the time came when I could give out that I was leaving at 11.00 hours on Sunday, January 29. When the day came there was a tropical cyclone northeast of Sydney, and it would have been advisable to delay my leaving. But I hated to do this. I think I have always sailed when I said I would. Max Hinchliffe advised me to get south as much as I could because of the storm, but foolishly I disregarded this excellent advice.

There was no storm in Sydney itself that morning—it was a fine, sunny day. And so, at 11.00 precisely, *Gipsy Moth IV* slipped her moorings and stood out to sea. Lord Casey, the Governor General, had presented me with three miniature bales of wool to be carried by *Gipsy Moth* to London and I reckoned that they were travelling by the smallest wool clipper that ever left Australia! . . .

In spite of the storm, radio conditions were good, and at 8 A.M. I had a good radio talk with Sheila which cheered me up. I was still sick from time to time, but slowly began to feel better, and gave myself some brandy, sugar and lemon, which I managed to keep down. The weather forecasts were bad with renewed cyclone warnings. This was Tropical Cyclone Diana, which was reported to be moving SE at about 20 mph. I tried to work out where it was in relation to me, and I reckoned that the worst of it would pass some 270 miles to the east of my noon position. That was something, but the whole area of the Tasman Sea was violently disturbed with winds from 40 to 60 knots, gusting up to 80 knots in squalls. There was nothing I could do about it. I did not worry over much, but just tried to exist until the storm passed. . . .

Gipsy Moth capsized on the night of Monday, January 30. My log notes briefly: "About 22.30. Capsize." Heavy weather continued throughout Tuesday, January 31, and I spent the day lying ahull, doing what I could to clear up. The electric bilge pump would not work, so I had to pump by hand, trying to repair the electric pump in the intervals of hand pumping. After I had cleaned the impeller the electric pump worked for a few minutes, but then sucked at an air lock. The bilge was still half-full, but gradually I got the water down. I streamed my remaining green warp in the hope that it would keep the yacht headed down-wind, but without any sails up the warp seemed to have no effect. So I hauled it back inboard and coiled it. The socket for the vane shaft of the self-steering gear was nearly off, so that had to be repaired, a dirty job which put me under water now and again. Thank God the water was warm! As I dealt with

these various jobs one after another, my spirits began to pick up.
I had been unbelievably lucky. The masts and rigging were all
intact, which I attributed largely to Warwick's rigging. I felt a
sense of loss that one of the big genoas had gone overboard, but
I could get on without it. I was upset at losing one of my drogues
and the 700 feet of drogue warp that went with it, for I had
intended to stream a drogue at the end of a long warp to slow
down *Gipsy Moth* and to keep her stern to the seas in Cape
Horner storms. Later, after I had pondered the details of my
capsize for many hours, I completely discarded the warp and
drogue idea. So the loss of those items was not as serious as I
thought at the time. . . .

At noon on Sunday, February 5, I was almost exactly halfway
between Sydney and Cape Maria Van Diemen, at the northwest tip of the North Island of New Zealand, 550 miles each
way. A week out, only 550 miles sailed. My log notes:

"550 miles in a week is my record for slow going. Of that 550,
I took four days to do 185 miles—an average of 46 miles per day!
However, I am still alive and kicking, which is the chief thing,
I suppose. . . .

"Wednesday, February 22, 19.25. I have just realized I have
only four bottles of gin left, enough for four weeks. My favorite
hard drink on this voyage. I reckon I have been pretty stupid
not to have brought plenty. I'll just have to ration it, and no hard
drinks at lunch. It might be worse—I might have none. . . .

"March 9, 11.40. Interrupted breakfast to reduce sail, because the lee deck was too often under water, rushing water,
indeed, and there was unnecessary strain on the boat. So
dropped genny stays'l and jib and hoisted spitfire in place, leaving only trysail and spitfire set. Bright sunny day but strong
breeze up to 40 k and some fierce waves. I turned 20° down-
wind, which eased things a lot.

"12.45. Still eating breakfast, which I last interrupted to get
a noon sun observation. Maybe it was a good thing I did so,
because the sky is totally overcast now a few minutes later.

"Day's run 179 miles. This is my 40th day at sea. I have sailed 5,083 miles and have 1,604 to go to the Horn. For the past 6 days I have been headed direct for the Horn and am now at latitude 47° 08′ S which is 311 miles nearer the South Pole. I put on my winter woollies this morning: wool shirt, long underfugs and thick socks, but it has turned out warm in the sun and with oilies keeping all air out I was parboiled on the foredeck. I shall need a pint of sea water tonight to keep the cramps away.". . .

I was lucky, and I got a sun fix at 09.22 . . . [one] morning. That put me about 40 miles southwest of the nearest rocks off Tierra del Fuego. I was 77 miles due west of the Ildefonso Islands, and 148½ miles from Cape Horn. . . .

At 10.43 [days later] I logged:

"I reckon I am east of Old Horn, but I can't get a bearing without going into the cockpit. Perhaps I had better, as I have kept my oilskins on. Still gusting over 50 knots." . . .

The wind had swung round to southwest and I heard later that someone aboard *Protector* had said the wind was 100 miles an hour when she left *Gipsy Moth*. I think that was a misquote, but six hours later I was in an angry storm, as if the Horn was letting me know what it could do if it tried. The anemometer only reads to 60 knots which, with the boat speed of 6 knots, amounted to at least 66 knots, but I would say it was gusting up to 75 knots and perhaps occasionally 85 knots or 100 mph. Powerful seas roared past, and breaking tops came rolling down onto me from the stern. I thanked God that I could run before it. My only fear was that the wind would continue to back, and make the land a lee shore. There was far more power in this sea than in the one that had capsized *Gipsy Moth* off Australia, and if I had had to stop running and lie ahull—well, it couldn't have been done. The worst time was at nightfall. In the increasing darkness the seas were just terrific. I admit I was frightened for a while. . . .

"18.05. That blow is over: it is fine mild weather. It makes me feel I have rounded the Horn at last, and in a few minutes I am going to crack a bottle of champagne to celebrate. After that I want a big sleep. The boat is under-canvassed but that must wait. By the way, as I passed the Horn at 16.07½ GMT March 20 I won my race with the sun; but only just—by 15.275 miles, the distance which the sun was still south of the Line." . . .

Doing my navigation that morning (March 25) I found that I had crossed the parallel of 50° S about midnight. The clipper captains, especially of the California clippers, considered this point very important, and always compared their times round the Horn from 50° S to 50° S. I crossed the 50th parallel west of the Horn in the Pacific at zero hours on March 12, and crossed it in the Atlantic at zero hours on March 25. That made 13 days.

My mileage tally for the week that saw me round the Horn was 1,106½, an average of 158 miles a day, or 6.58 knots. This was the fifth week in succession that *Gipsy Moth* had sailed over 1,000 miles in the week: 5,230½ miles in 35 days, an average of 149.4 miles per day. These distances, of course, are run over straight lines between noon positions, and do not include tacks or digressions. . . .

On Sunday, March 26, I logged: "Hot news! At noon today I passed half way!" I had sailed 7,673 miles from Sydney, and the distance along the Clipper Way to Plymouth was 7,634 miles by my measurement. I started plotting the different sailing routes up the two Atlantics recommended by the Admiralty's *Ocean Passages of the World* for March, April and May. . . .

On April 15 it looked as if I was in the Trade Wind at last, after several disappointing false starts. That night I saw the Plough constellation for the first time on the voyage home, and it gave me a thrill.

Next day *Gipsy Moth* passed the 10,000-mile mark from Sydney. I wrote:

"I ought to be cock-a-hoop, but instead I feel a little desperate, apprehensive and homesick. I still have 5,200 miles to go [5,500 had I known it], so I have only done two-thirds of the passage. Such hundreds of things can go wrong in such a distance. I seem to have been a long time away from home, and home seems a long time away. This is only weakness, of course. Between whiles I am having a thrilling sail. The crescent moon is dead ahead looking in through the cabin window at me." . . .

TRADE WINDS AND DOLDRUMS

I crossed the equator at 03.30 on Monday morning, April 24, but it was too early in the day to celebrate. The Line was succeeded by Doldrums, long periods of calm, and then light airs coming from all round the compass. There was heavy rain between whiles. . . .

On May 7 I was hailed by the *Esso Winchester,* the first ship I had seen since Cape Horn. To my disgust I found that this first contact with people was making me tremble, but it reminded me that three months' solitude is strong medicine. One may behave as usual, but for a while one's feelings are changed. . . .

On May 17 a school of black fish (pilot whales), surfacing lazily, went past astern. I next saw them a mile to the north. It was hot and I felt languid and tired, and off color. The radio telephone worried me—I wanted to be free of everything but the job of sailing. My arm [injured earlier], which was still more painful that day, was also having a bad effect. Unfortunately, it had had two nasty jabs the day before while handling the pole in the shemozzle.

In the small hours of next morning I saw a motor vessel, bearing 255°, overtaking me. I had had a good sleep, and my arm seemed slightly better, though the pain had extended in a line up to the armpit, which I supposed was the poison reaching the gland there. The motor vessel was the *Sea Huntress,* which the *Sunday Times* hired to hunt for me. I wished that I could be left alone to get on with my job. . . .

On Sunday morning, May 28, I logged:

"Thunder showers. Too much trimming for too little distance. *Wind wind wind, where art thou*? This business is quite a strain. I wish I could get into port. It looks as if there is no chance today."

At noon I counted 13 ships around, including five naval vessels escorting me. I was in a quandary, with the light breeze blowing, interspersed with calms; I could improve the speed by poling out a big sail and it seemed that this would enable me to reach Plymouth before dark, but it would be at the price of considerable extra effort, and would result in my arriving even more tired than I was, with the likelihood of a terrific strain ahead of me. On the other hand, if I did not speed up, I was likely to be out at sea for another night, and that would be a great strain too, with all the ships and boats around me.

At 15.20 the huge aircraft carrier HMS *Eagle* passed close by, with her crew lining the deck and giving *Gipsy Moth* three cheers. I dipped my ensign in salute. This was a great honor, which I found most moving. It must surely be unique in the history of the British Navy for a warship with a complement as big as the population of a small town to salute so ceremoniously a ship with a crew of one!

Presently, when a minesweeper followed suit, I got a little nervous—I could picture myself dashing out to the stern and dipping the ensign, which is hoisted to the top of the mizzen mast, at frequent intervals for the rest of the day!

Late in the afternoon the breeze quickened a little, and at 16.40 by my ship's time I was 13 miles off Plymouth Breakwater, and knew that I *would* get in that night.

At 20.56 I passed the breakwater, and Colonel Jack Odling Smee, the Rear-Commodore of the Royal Western Yacht Club, fired a finishing gun from his yacht anchored off the breakwater, a sign for a beacon to be lit on Drake's Island.

Gipsy Moth had completed her passage home of 15,517 miles in 119 days, an average speed of 130 miles per day. The whole voyage of 29,630 miles had taken just nine months and one day from Plymouth to Plymouth of which the sailing time was 226 days. Perhaps I might add that, with eight log books filled up, I had also written more than 200,000 words.

Epilogue

Francis Chichester was knighted soon after that. His achievements:
1. *The fastest voyage by a small yacht around the world.*
2. *Longest passage without a port of call—15,500 miles.*
3. *Twice the distance made by any other solo voyager before a port of call.*
4. *Broke the record twice for solo-sailor's weekly run by over 100 miles.*
5. *Established record for weekly run—1400 miles.*
6. *Twice exceeded the singlehanded speed record for a long passage. Nance's was 122 ½ miles per day for 53 days.* Gipsy Moth's *speeds were 131 ¾ miles per day for 107 days, and 130 ¼ miles per day for 119 days.*

THE BOMBARD STORY

ALAIN BOMBARD

The story of Alain Bombard is the story of a man who endured great hardship not in order to secure his own survival but to inspire others with the courage and the will to survive under similar circumstances.

Bombard, a young French doctor, had become deeply concerned by the number of lives lost at sea. His studies and experiments led him to believe that it is possible for anyone to survive in an open boat for a considerable time, obtaining nourishment from the sea itself, from fish and plankton and seawater in limited quantities, and that, therefore, many of those who perish each year at sea must die not of starvation, but of fear and panic.

In the early 1950s, to put his theories to the test, Bombard sailed alone across the Atlantic in a small rubber craft. The only food he took with him was in a sealed container, and in spite of the fact that he spent 65 days at sea this container remained unopened until he reached land. In fact, his diary proves that of all the dangers which beset him on his lonely journey, starvation was the most remote.

The example of Alain Bombard will be remembered among those of the many scientists who have risked and often given their own lives that their experiments might save the lives of others.

"Land! Land!" is the cry of the castaway when he sights the first coast. My cry on November 11th was "Rain! Rain!"

I had noticed for some time that the surface of the sea had become strangely calm, exactly as if it were sleeked down with oil, and suddenly I realized why: "Rain! Here comes the rain," I cried aloud.

I stripped ready for it, so that I could wash all the salt off my body, and then sat down on one of the floats. I stretched out the tent on my knees, and held between my legs an inflatable rubber mattress, capable of holding some fifteen gallons of water. I waited. Like the sound of a soda syphon, monstrously magnified, I heard advancing from far away the noise of water beating on water. I must have waited nearly twenty minutes, watching the slow approach of this manna from heaven. The waves were flattened under the weight of the rain, and the wind buffeted me as the squall hit the boat. The cloud passed over slowly, writhing with the vertical turbulence of a small cyclone. I was drenched in a tropical downpour, which rapidly filled the tent sheet and made it sag with the weight between my knees. I plunged my head in it and as quickly spat the water out again. It was impregnated with salt from the tent and I let it all spill overboard. At the second fill, although the water tasted strongly of rubber, it was like nectar. I washed myself voluptuously. The squall did not last long, but the rainfall was tremendous. Not only did I drink my fill that day, but I was able to store three or four gallons in my rubber mattress. I was going to have a gurgling pillow, but each night my reserve of water was going to renew my hopes for the next day. Even if I had nothing to eat, even if I caught no fish, I at least had something to drink.

For three weeks I had not had a drop of fresh water, only the liquid I pressed from my fish, but my reactions were perfectly normal, just the marvelous sensation of swallowing a real drink at last. My skin was still in good order, although much affected by the salt, my mucous membranes had not dried, and my urine had remained normal in quantity, smell and color. I had proved conclusively that a castaway could live for three weeks (and

even longer, because I could have continued perfectly well)
without fresh water. It is true that Providence was to spare me
the ordeal of having to rely again on the flat, insipid fish juice.
From that day on I always had enough rainwater to slake my
thirst. It sometimes seemed as if my stock was about to run out,
but a shower always came in time.

I found that it was impossible to wash the salt out of my
clothes and bedding, and I had to remain until the end "a man
of saltwater" (as the Polynesians say of people who live off the
sea), completely encrusted with it until the day of my arrival.

The day of the rain brought me both pleasure and perturba-
tion. The pleasure consisted in a new sort of bird, an attractive
creature called, in English, I believe, a white-tailed tropic bird,
and which the French call a *paille-cul*. It looks like a white dove
with a black beak and has a long quill in its tail, which, with an
impertinent air, it uses as an elevator. I rummaged quickly for
my raft book, written for the use of castaways, and read that the
appearance of this bird did not necessarily mean that one was
near land. But as it could only come from the American continent, being completely unknown in the Old World, it was a
good sign. For the first time, I had met a bird which came,
without a shadow of doubt, from my destination.

This pleasant interlude was succeeded at about two o'clock in
the afternoon by twelve hours of terror, which lasted until two
the next morning. Just as I was peacefully reading a little Aes-
chylus, there was a violent blow on the rudder: "That's another
shark," I thought, and looked up. What I saw was a large
swordfish of undeniably menacing aspect. He was following the
dinghy at a distance of about twenty feet, seemingly in a rage,
his dorsal fin raised like hackles. In one of his feints round the
boat, he had collided with my rudder oar. I found I had a
determined enemy. If I only succeeded in wounding him he
would surely attack again, and that would be the end of *L'Hérétique*. What was worse, as I was hurriedly getting my harpoon
ready, a clumsy movement knocked it into the sea. It was my

last one. Now I was disarmed. I fixed my pocket knife on to my underwater gun as a makeshift bayonet, determined to sell my life dearly if he attacked in earnest.

This intolerable anxiety lasted twelve long hours. As night fell I could follow the swordfish's movements by his luminous wake and the noise his dorsal fin made cutting the water. Several times his back bumped the underside of the dinghy, but he still seemed a little afraid of me. He never approached from ahead, and every time he came at me he changed course at the last moment before striking the floats. I came to believe that he was frightened, probably as frightened as I was. Every living creature possesses some means of defense, but it must perturb an attacker not to know what it is. In the early hours of the morning his wake disappeared, but I spent a sleepless night.

One of the lulls in this encounter brought a minor relief, which I interpreted as a message from the land. It was one of those little glass floats used on fishing nets, encrusted with little shellfish, cirripedia and other sorts of barnacle. It had clearly been in the water a long time, but it was a sign of human life.

It was an exhausting day, and by the time it was over I was utterly miserable. It rained so hard during the night that I thought I was going to have too much fresh water, after having gone without it for so long. I wrote: "It would really be too much if I drowned in fresh water, but that is what is going to happen if this downpour goes on. I have enough for a month. My God, what a cloudburst! What is more, the sea is rising. A pale sun poked through this morning, but it is still raining."

Another excitement was what I took to be my first clump of Sargasso seaweed. In fact, it was a magnificent jellyfish, the float blue and violet, of the type known as a Portuguese man-of-war. Its long treacherous filaments, hanging to a considerable depth, can cause dangerous stings, which often develop into ulcers.

I realized after one or two wakeful nights how essential it was to get a good sleep: "Forty-eight hours without sleep, and I am utterly depressed; the ordeal is really beginning to get me down. Moreover, the sea is infested with tunny and swordfish. I can see them leaping all round me. I do not mind the tunny and the birds so much, but the swordfish are a real menace. Am making good speed, but would willingly add another five or six days to the voyage if I could rest up in comparative calm. This dark, forbidding sea has a depressing effect." It really seemed as if the sea was in mourning. It was as black as ink, flecked from time to time by a white crest, which the plankton made luminous by night. It looked like an evening dress with occasional white flowers, or a Japanese mourning robe. Not a star to be seen and the low sky seemed about to crush me. I realized the full meaning of the term "heavy weather"; it felt like a physical weight on my shoulders.

At five o'clock on November 12th I noted: "Rain and yet more rain, this is more than I can stand. But I wonder if I am not nearer the coast than I think, as there are several more birds. There are ten round me at the same time, and my bird book says that more than six means that one is not more than a hundred or two hundred miles from the coast." Little did I think that I was only just over a hundred miles away from the Cape Verde Islands.

During the nights of November 12th and 13th, I had another visit from a shark, or at least so I hoped. There was no way of telling whether it was a shark or a swordfish. Every time a shark appeared during the day, I felt perfectly safe. I gave it the ritual clout on the nose and off it went. But during the night, fearing that one of those devilish creatures might spear me with his sword, I was no longer able to be so bold. I had to remain watchfully awake, trying to identify the intruder, and waiting wide-eyed for it to make off. Sleep was effectively banished. And often it seemed that sharks or other creatures were playing some sort of ball-game during the night with my dinghy, without my daring to interfere.

It was still raining in torrents. Under such a deluge I was

obliged to stretch the tent right over my head, but it formed great pockets of water which trickled down through the gaps. After a certain time, the weight threatened to break the guy ropes, and I had to push from underneath to spill the water overboard. It must be difficult to realize the sacrifice involved for a castaway in thus jettisoning his reserve of fresh water. Even without sharks and swordfish, sleep had become practically impossible. The rain thundered down and every quarter of an hour or so I had to heave it overboard. An unbelievable quantity of water fell on the tent and trickled through every crevice.

I began to believe, in a confused sort of way, in the active hostility of certain inanimate objects. I might decide to write up the log or work out some calculations. I would sit down, with a pencil ready at hand. I only needed to turn round for ten seconds, and it found some means of disappearing. It was like a mild form of persecution mania, although up till then I had always been able to meet such annoyances with good humor, thinking of the similar misfortunes suffered by the *Three Men in a Boat.*

"*Friday, November 14th.* The last forty-eight hours have been the worst of the voyage. I am covered with little spots and my tongue is coated. I do not like the look of things at all. The storm has been short and violent. Was obliged to put out the sea anchor for several hours, but hoisted sail again at about 9.30. Raining in sheets and everything soaked through. Morale still fairly good, but I am starting to get physically tired of the perpetual wetness, which there is no sun to dry. I do not think I have lost a great deal of time, but it is impossible to determine my latitude as I can see neither sun nor stars, and another of these confounded rainstorms is blowing up from the horizon. The sea is calmer, but yesterday I shipped plenty. They say, 'fine weather follows rain.' I can hardly wait for it."

During the night a thunderous wave, catching me by stern, carried me along at great speed and then flooded *L'Hérétique,* at the same time breaking my rudder oar. The dinghy immediately turned broadside on and my sail started to flap in a sinister manner, straining at my rough stitches. I plunged forward to gather it in, but stumbled against the tent and tore a great rent near the top of one of the poles. There would be no way of mending it properly and it happened just as I had to battle for life with the waves. I threw out both my sea anchors. Docilely, *L'Hérétique* turned her stern to my normal course and faced up to her assailants. By this time I was at the end of my strength and, accepting all the risks, I decided that sleep was the first necessity. I fastened up the tent as close as I could and made up my mind to sleep for twenty-four hours, whatever the weather did and whatever happened.

The squalls continued for another ten hours, during which my eggshell craft behaved admirably. But the danger was not yet passed. The worst moments came after the wind had dropped, while the sea continued to rage. The wind seemed to enforce a sort of discipline on the sea, propelling the waves without giving them time to break: left to themselves, they were much less disciplined. They broke with all their force in every direction, overwhelming everything in their path.

"Saturday, November 15th, 13.30. Taking advantage of the rain to do a little writing. Have only two rudder oars left. Hope they will hold out. Rain has been coming down in torrents since ten o'clock yesterday evening, no sign of the sun; am wet through. Everything is soaked and I have no means of drying a thing, my sleeping bag looks like a wet sack. No hope of taking my position. The weather was so bad during the night that I wondered for a time if I had not drifted into the Doldrums. Fortunately there is no doubt that the trade wind is still with me. Making good time, almost too fast for comfort. Still worried about the sail. When will the weather clear up? There was one patch of blue sky in the west, but the wind is from the east. Perhaps tomorrow will be better, but I am going to have another thick night. About seven o'clock this morning an aircraft

flew over me quite low. Tried to signal it, but my torch would not work. First sign of human life since November 3rd, hope there will be more. Sky to the west now clearing rapidly, difficult to understand why."

There was a sort of battle in the sky the whole day between the two fronts of good and bad weather. I called it the fight between the blue and the black. It started with the appearance in the west of a little patch of blue, no bigger than a gendarme's cap, as the French song has it, and there seemed little hope of it growing. The black clouds, impenetrable as ink, seemed fully conscious of their power, and marched in serried ranks to attack the tiny blue intruder, but the blue patch seemed to call up reinforcements on its wings, and in a few hours to the south and north, that is to say to my left and right, several more blue patches had appeared, all seemingly about to be engulfed in the great black flood advancing towards them. But where the clouds concentrated on frontal attacks, the blue of the sky used infiltration tactics, breaking up the mass of black until the good weather predominated. By four o'clock in the afternoon its victory was clear. "Thank God for the sun! I am covered with little spots, but the sun is back." Little did I know that the most troublesome part of my voyage was about to begin.

I had not the faintest idea where I was. With no sun for three days I was in a state of complete ignorance, and on Sunday the 16th when I got my sextant ready, I was in a fever of apprehension. By a miracle I had not drifted much to the south. I was still on latitude 16° 59', which passes to the north of Guadeloupe. That vital point was settled, but my boat looked like a battlefield. My hat had blown off in the storm and all I now had as protection for my head was a little white floppy thing, made out of waterproofed linen, quite inadequate in such a climate. The tent was torn in two places and although the dinghy seemed to have suffered no damage, everything in it was drenched. Even after the long sunny days which were now to come, the night dew continued to reimpregnate my warm clothes and sleeping bag, so I was never again to know a dry night until I touched land.

A disturbing incident then showed that I could not afford to relax my vigilance for one moment. During the storm, I had tried to protect the after part of L'Hérétique from the breaking waves by trailing a large piece of rubberized cloth fixed firmly to the ends of my two floats. This seemed to divert the force of the waves as they broke behind me. Even though the storm had died down, I saw no point in removing this protection. But the following night, a frightful noise brought me out of my sleeping bag at one bound. My protective tail was no longer there. The piece of cloth had been torn away. I checked anxiously that the floats had not been damaged and that they were still firmly inflated. Some creature which I never saw, probably attracted by the vivid yellow color of the cloth which hung down between the floats, had torn it off by jumping out of the water. This it had done with such precision that there was no other visible sign of its attack.

Like the boat, I too had taken a buffeting. I was much weakened and every movement made me terribly tired, rather like the period after my long fast in the Mediterranean. I was much thinner, but was more worried about the state of my skin. My whole body was covered with tiny red spots. At first they were little more than surface discolorations, not perceptible to the touch, but in a day or two they became hard lumps that finally developed into pustules. I was mortally afraid of a bad attack of boils, which, in the condition I was in, would have had serious consequences. The pain alone would have proved unbearable and I would no longer have been able to sit or lie down.

The only medicament I had to treat such an outbreak was mercurochrome, which made me look as if I was covered in blood. During the night the pain became very bad and I could not bear anything in contact with my skin. The least little abrasion seemed to turn septic and I had to disinfect them all very carefully. The skin under my nails was all inflamed, and small

pockets of pus, very painful, formed under half of them. I had
to lance them without an anaesthetic. I could probably have
used some of the penicillin I had on board, but I wanted to keep
up my medical observations with a minimum of treatment for
as long as I could stand it. My feet were peeling in great strips
and in three days I lost the nails from four toes.

I would never have been able to hold out if the deck had not
been made of wood, which I regard as an essential piece of
equipment in a life-raft. Without it I would have developed
gangrene or, at the very least, serious arterial trouble.

For the time being my ailments were still localized. My blood
pressure remained good and I was still perspiring normally. In
spite of that, I greeted with relief the victorious sun which
appeared on the 16th, expecting it to cure the effects of the
constant humidity which I had endured. I did not know that the
sun was to cause even worse ordeals during the cruel twenty-
seven days which were to follow.

The castaway must never give way to despair, and should
always remember, when things seem at their worst, that "something will turn up" and his situation may be changed. But neither should he let himself become too hopeful; it never does to
forget that however unbearable an ordeal may seem, there may
be another to come which will efface the memory of the first.
If a toothache becomes intolerable, it might almost seem a relief
to exchange it for an earache. With a really bad pain in the ear,
the memory of the toothache becomes a distinctly lesser evil.
The best advice that I can give is that whether things go well
or ill, the castaway must try to maintain a measure of detach-
ment. The days of rain had been bad enough, but what followed, in spite of the rosy future the sun at first seemed to
promise, was to seem much worse.

WHOM THE SEA HAS TAKEN

WILLIAM WILLIS

William Willis, known as the "Thoreau of the Sea," learned about ships in the port of Hamburg, Germany, where he was born before the turn of the century. He went to sea at 15, sailing square riggers around Cape Horn. Eventually becoming an American, he worked at all the tough trades, including logging, dock-walloping, prospecting for oil, construction-ganging and oil drilling. But the seas of the world, always his youthful and middle-aged fancy, called him back to the ships, especially to rafts, as the lonely voyager. He preferred the green and blue oceans to the crowding cities for his physical and spiritual adventures as a uniquely individualistic solo sailor.

He wrote many books, including *Hell, Hail and Hurricanes,* the story of a solo raft voyage that took him, in 1954, from Peru to American Samoa, or more than 7000 miles on seven balsa logs. He established a record as the hermit of the seas in distance traveled and in time spent alone. Ten years later he was to go by raft again, from Peru to Australia, taking 204 days to float and sail 11,000 miles.

Following are sections of his last book, *Whom the Sea Has Taken,* in which William Willis starts his voyage from Peru to Australia. With two cats aboard for companionship, he says good-bye to his wife, Teddy, and is pulled out to sea by a tug.

Thus begins William Willis's sea odyssey, at the age of 71.

The piers of the base were crowded with onlookers, and the ships, from truck to deck, lined with blue-jackets. Crowds had come out from Lima—ambassadors, consuls, men of different embassies, and the officers of the U.S. Navy mission who had assisted me from the day of my arrival. I was ready to sail. It was two thirty in the afternoon, July 4, 1963.

A launch pulled the raft out of the slip and 'longside of the *Rios,* a big navy salvage tug which had taken me out for the trial run. Three sailors jumped down to the raft from its deck, and the tow-line was made fast. One of the sailors had a walkie-talkie, and they were to stay with me till I was turned loose the next morning about fifty miles off the coast. . . .

I stood by the wheel as the raft plowed through the gray water. Fishing boats were coming in through the breakwater loaded with their catch, and oilskin-clad men were waving, while small boats followed in our wake and crowded close for a last look at my strange craft and perhaps at the equally strange *Navegante Solitario.* The clouds hung low, almost down to the top of my mast, and the air was heavy, the wind raw and cold. I felt no joy at coming to grips with my big experiment of proving that I had conquered old age, for the picture of Teddy was before my eyes, standing at the end of the pier less than a mile behind me, a small frail figure huddled against the wind and waving a handkerchief, her face wet with tears.

"Oh, Bill," she had said, "shall I go to dinner tonight with Dell? She wants me to. She's going to drive me back to the hotel and wants to be with me all day and then wants me to sleep in her house, so I wouldn't be alone. What shall I do? I don't want to stay with anybody today—I want to go right back to the hotel and—and . . ." Her face was quivering, fighting back tears.

"Lie down and cry, I know. Do that, do that, Teddy," I said and added, "and don't forget: I'll be in touch with you all the time—you know what I mean." Then we parted.

We were at sea. The big tug was wallowing ahead, big as a battleship. The grayness of sea and sky was dense, almost like

a solid, and visibility was less than a mile. Hour after hour went
by. At dusk I went forward and tied a lantern to the jibboom.
A powerful floodlight already lighted up the stern of the tug.
Suddenly the tug whistled, let go the line, and I was on my way
to Australia alone. . . .

> Logbook entry, September 11, 1963
>   Long: 140° 10′ west
>   Lat: 03° 22′ south
>   Course: west by south
>   Wind: southeast
>   4570 miles from Callao

Checking my position on the chart, I found that I was 330
miles north of Nuku Hiva in the Marquesas—much further
north than I liked—but the wind had been strong and consis-
tently from southeast, and it was hard to get back south. On my
1954 voyage I passed the 140th meridian in latitude 5 degrees
38 minutes, only 190 miles from Nuku Hiva. I had considered
the voyage half over then and started to level off for the final
stretch to Pago Pago, the destination I had cleared for, and
changed course to west southwest. This time I was handicapped
with almost useless rudders and looked at my charts with increasing apprehension as I saw the atolls and reefs ahead of me,
though for the next few thousand miles I anticipated little trouble. The nearest reef ahead now was the Filippo Reef, approximately six hundred or eight hundred miles away in latitude 5
degrees 30 minutes south, with breakers reported as far south
as 6 degrees 20 minutes. I hoped to pass to the south of it, unless
the southerly wind continued and made it impossible. . . .

Fresh food had been one of the main problems on board since
the first log raft or canoe left a shore to tackle the unknown
beyond the horizon. Scurvy, caused by lack of fresh food, is
perhaps the most dreadful of all mankind's diseases. In a fully
developed case a human body turns to loathsome, red-flecked
mud, screaming at the slightest movement. Cholera, yellow

fever, all the big plagues which have devastated the earth are merciful compared to this scourge of the sea.

Personally I think that, besides lemon or lime juice, a daily drink of perhaps half a cup of seawater would keep scurvy from breaking out. I had also read of an American whaling-ship captain of the old days who kept scurvy from his crew by giving them a daily ration of sauerkraut of which he had several barrels. The big Galápagos turtles taken on board by whaling ships in hundreds and kept alive also did their share in keeping seamen healthy.

For my lunch today I had dehydrated vegetable soup with dolphin meat and thickened with wheat germ. Sometimes I made the same dish with a grated potato or a broken-up ship's biscuit. . . .

> Logbook entry, October 5, 1963
>> Long: 155° 16' west
>> Lat: 10° 16' south
>> Course: southwest by west
>> Wind: north-northeast

Out 3 months today and covered appr. 5,700 miles. Weather continues bad. Don't seem to know the Pacific of 1954.

I had thrown out my fishing line in the early dawn, and a dolphin took it. The fear and fury of the hooked fish fairly leaped from the line into me, as if I held its body with my bare hands, and I had a time pulling it in. When it was about ten feet away, I saw another dolphin near it—a bull with a tremendous head. First I thought the two fish had been fighting, then realized that the other was its mate and trying to help it. I swung it on board in all its beauty and saw the gasping mouth with the hook in the upper jaw, the big, limpid eyes full of agony, and its mate, utterly maddened, leaping against the pontoon trying to follow it to the deck. After I had landed it, I stepped back, letting it smash about till the hook was out of its jaw, for I had decided to spare it. The next moment it was back in the sea and speeding away beside its mate in a mass of foam, a piece of upper jaw left on the hook. When we were on our West Indies sloop, Teddy never ate of a dolphin if she had seen its eyes after it was hooked or when it lay dying on deck, its gorgeous colors turned gray. . . .

I had hooked a shark and, after shooting it, hoisted it on board, cut out the liver, and ate quite a hunk raw and still warm, Polynesian style. I also boiled part of it. The shark was a six-footer with a large, fine liver. Some shark livers are full of vitamins, while others have little. I tried to get my cats Kiki and Aussie to eat some, but they turned their noses away and into the wind. My stomach felt a little jumpy afterwards but settled after a few cups of hot coffee. The shark had a few fish in its stomach that I hadn't seen around the raft, probably from some reef. I was almost 14 degrees south. The course I had originally mapped out was along the 12th parallel, but I was quite re-signed now to sail between the Tongas and Samoan islands should the wind hold. The Tongas are a great mass of tiny islands and atolls, many of which are uninhabited. It is an inde-pendent domain which was then ruled by a queen, and its people are supposed to be friendly. . . .

About two o'clock in the afternoon the sky had begun to look bad, but I kept the mainsail up. The wind increased gradually, and when a few hours later I touched the mizzen behind me, it was as hard as a sheet of iron, and I doubted whether I could get the big sail down without having it torn. I kept racing before it until three explosions beneath me, one quickly following the other, told me that three of my centerboards had snapped off. The raft swung into the wind, and the sail went aback with a blast that stopped the raft and began beating against the mast with a fury which threatened to bring down the whole rigging. I threw the lashings over the wheel and jumped forward just as the sail was ripped from top to bottom. Expecting to have nothing left but a mass of shreds, I lowered away. The raft now swung before the wind again, and the yard was blown forward all the way to the jibboom, and I dived into the sail, thinking I had tangled with wild horses. After a long struggle, I managed to secure what was left and lashed the yard to the legs of the mast. Then I set the jib. . . .

About an hour after dark I saw a light aft, about half a point to starboard. At first I thought it was a ship, for it seemed to be steady; then I saw that it flashed, though the heaving sea prevented an accurate count and therefore its identification. Checking my chart, I thought that it was probably the light on the western tip of Tutuila, American Samoa. It seemed to be about five miles off. This gave me a pretty good idea of my position. It also told me that I was sailing on the edge of disaster. . . .

By morning, after a terrible night, the sky was still threatening. Slowly I approached the island, which sometimes, amid the driven clouds and squalls, showed the clear outline of summits.

I had hoisted the American flag upside down as a signal of distress, in order to draw attention to the raft and if possible have the pilot boat come out to show me the way through the reef into the harbor. But was there a lookout station? When I went up on the mast again, I could make out what I thought was a break in the reef and so most likely the entrance to the lagoon of Apia. The wind and current were slowly pushing me down the coast to the west, away from the town, though with my mainsail up I could have held a course for the opening. . . .

The wind has carried me three or four miles down the coast, and Apia is lost behind a palm-studded little headland. The reef is quite close. The time has almost come. I have to go straight in, for to my right it is breaking house-high, with reef after reef extending for miles toward Upolu's big sister island, Savai'i, with its six-thousand-foot-high mountains just visible among the clouds that have piled up around them dark and heavy. . . .

Yard by yard I'm coming in. The reef bares its black wall of boulders, after each sea drops. A big comber picks up the raft, flings it forward, and then drops it. For a moment it lies helpless, then is lifted again and flung forward. I stare at the foul wall of the reef in front of me. Another sea picks up the raft and—I hang on to the wheel, my eyes darting up to the mast to see which way to jump should it fall.

Foam blots out everything as we strike. The shock seems to dismember the raft, and I am smashed against the spokes. We are hammered on the boulders by the seas and seem to disintegrate. Raft and cabin are engulfed in foam. All the centerboards, though only a few feet deep in the water, have broken off, and some of the deck planks have been ripped out with them. Suddenly the bow comes up and slowly drops again. A heavy sea breaks over the stern. The convulsions continue. I wonder that the mast remains standing. Then the raft begins to move from side to side. A sea lifts it and flings it ahead. It lands solid, on all three pontoons, then is lifted again and once more smashed down and lies with a list to starboard. Another sea wrenches us clear and pushes us through the foam. Again we stop, bump along a few yards, then slide forward; after another shock and lift by a sea coming over the stern, we sink almost gently down. We are over the reef and in the lagoon.

I am still at the wheel, and the sails fill with wind, and we head for the shore about four hundred yards away. We bump over boulders and hang up, but the seas coming over the reef push us clear. Twenty-five yards from the shore, which is guarded by huge coral blocks, I run forward and drop the anchor, then lower jib and mizzen. The raft swings around. After 130 days of solitude and sailing approximately seventy-five hundred miles, the raft has landed. Kiki and Aussie are on deck. "Well, little fellows, we made it," I say and lift them high up and tell them to take a look at the scenery.

Apia is hidden behind the wooded headland, and I see no sign of life in the lagoon. Dusk is setting in. After a while I notice a skiff driven by an outboard motor come out of a nearby bay with a man and woman in it. I wave and shout, and they see me and after hesitating a bit come 'longside.

"Glad to see you," I say, overcome with joy at seeing human beings again. "I've just come from South America. . . ."

They stare at me, and I wonder if they speak English. "You speak English, don't you?" I ask.

"Yes, we speak English," the man says in a cultured voice, still keeping a few feet away from the side of the raft, probably not quite trusting this half-naked, sun-scorched, and white-bearded fellow on such strange-looking craft and making such a crazy statement.

I tell them who I am and ask them to notify the authorities at once—and also a radio station, should there be one, for I want the news of my arrival to get on the air as quickly as possible so that Teddy knows.

The skiff turns around and with racing motor heads back to the bay from which it came. I am alone again. The sun has set, and the mangroves cast dark shadows over the raft. Everything is quiet and so strange. The man had introduced himself as the Reverend Mr. Maddox, head of the Methodist Mission of Upolu, and the lady as his wife. I clear up the deck and feed my little shipmates, then open a can of beans and eat standing by the wheel as if that was my ordained place. I feel suddenly lonely, as if something has been taken out of my life. . . .

On landing in Samoa in November 1963, Willis discovered that he was developing a strangulated hernia, for which an operation was necessary. He left the raft with the Samoan authorities, expecting to return and continue his solo raft voyage to Australia in a few months, and flew to New York. But he did not have the operation, talking the doctor out of it. He returned to Samoa six months later to continue the voyage.

We rejoin Willis after he has been at sea for weeks on his rebuilt raft, on July 25, 1964. Destination—Australia.

Logbook entry, July 25, 1964
Long: 174° 43′ east
Lat: 17° 45′ south

I had tried to get south and clear the southeastern tip of New Caledonia for a straight run to Sydney, but bad weather and head winds again and again forced me back north and to the west. Finally the wind assumed gale force, blowing straight from the south. I had pored over my charts in the wildest night since leaving Apia, while the raft seemed to be coming apart, and realized that there was no chance to continue on my course. I had run north, in the opposite direction, to keep from being blown on the rocks of the New Hebrides. That had been two days ago. . . .

It was just a few minutes after midnight of August 19, my seventy-first birthday, and I had been thinking what a pleasant surprise it would have been for Teddy to get the news on that very day that I was still alive and sailing.

While I was kneeling beside my stove, the cabin became suddenly filled with light streaming through the after porthole. The steamer that had been following me was coming up astern, its big searchlight full on the raft and flooding it with its glare. By the time I had hoisted the American flag, it was ranging 'longside with such speed and so close that I was afraid of being run down.

"Who are you?" a voice hailed me from the bridge.

"Captain Willis on the raft *Age Unlimited*," I answered.

"What do you want?"

"Just report me, that's all."

That same day Teddy received the following telegram from the Australian Consulate General in New York:

MRS. WILLIAM WILLIS

AUSTRALIAN AUTHORITIES ADVISE MASTER OF BARON JEDBURGH REPORTS HAVING SIGHTED RAFT AGE UNLIMITED 12.15 AM AUG 19TH POSITION 15° 44' SOUTH 159° 45' EAST

My mind was benumbed—all enthusiasm, all zest and eagerness for living had gone out of it. Perhaps I had been through too much on the voyage, and the last days on the reef had finished me. I was just a sailor now, staring into the darkness with little left but the aim to bring his ship and himself to a safe landing. This change had come about during the previous night after I had cleared the first two reefs and was in the Inner Passage. Standing by the wheel then, I had thought that I would reach Australia some time in the morning, and the voyage would be over. I had envisaged this with great distinctness. I had seen Australians come on board and greet me, quiet, friendly men and full of understanding. So strongly and deeply had this vision of my landing and being safe become implanted on my mind that it became a reality—not permanently of course but implanted so deeply in my subconscious that it came back again and again in moments of danger. The first time I became aware of this was when I awoke to see the raft almost in the breakers of the last reef. Then I saw the Australians, just as they had come on board to greet me, on the raft crowding around me, and I became angry that they didn't jump in and help but left me to struggle alone. The next moment, of course, my head cleared. In my subconscious however the Australians remained, appearing again and again and always under similar circumstances—when the work seemed almost more than I could handle.

I remembered I had had similar experiences, extending over several months during the first part of my voyage, from Callao to Samoa, when my mother and Teddy appeared to me. . . .

Suddenly I jumped up, for I had seen a light. I had been asleep and seen it in my sleep but didn't realize it in the suddenness of my awakening. I felt so certain that I had actually seen it that it took quite a while to convince me I had been dreaming. I just couldn't get my thoughts together. . . . Then it came again. Sometimes I didn't see it for a few minutes, but it always came back. Was it a ship perhaps or a fishing boat bobbing up and

down in the seas. The night was like a cave, but the tiny light
came through as clear as a star. I lashed the wheel and climbed
into the rigging and finally made out that it was a lighthouse.
There were four flashes and then a stop for eight seconds before
the flashes returned. If I had had a chart, I would have been able
to identify it and know my position, but now I only knew that
there was danger ahead. But where was the danger—to the
right or to the left?

Four flashes, then eight seconds of darkness—I could see it
now from the deck. I swung the raft over to the right, merely
on a hunch, but after sailing for about twenty minutes brought
it back till I had the light about two points off the starboard
bow. . . .

Suddenly during the eight seconds of darkness, I saw the
island, sprawling back in the sea beside me—sinister, terrible,
and strangely close—before the light began swinging around
again. I pulled the wheel hard over and stood as if transfixed,
staring into the night, feeling helpless in the grip of powers
beyond my control. Something that would destroy the raft and
me was taking shape in that terrible darkness before my very
eyes, and I was helpless. Suddenly the light went out. I held my
breath almost paralyzed by terror. The light didn't come back,
and then I realized that I had sailed into the obscure sector, the
ultimate warning that rocks were ahead.

The raft struck with shattering force, reeled, and went into
what I can only call convulsions, bounding up and down like
something demented. It had been hurled high up on rocks and
was pounded by the seas. It was a life-and-death struggle among
rocks and cataracts and the hurricane fury of the wind. I flashed
my light over the side and saw a large, bulging rock on which
the raft lay in its throes. Beyond, on the starboard side, were
masses of jagged, high rocks standing like tombstones, while
ahead was a solid wall of still larger rocks; to the left I could see
only breakers. . . .

I was hanging on, waiting for the raft to become a heap of

smashed iron. It was, at times, like hanging on to the inner edge of an exploding crater. Again and again my hands were torn loose from the ropes, which I hung on to with such force that it threatened to break my fingers, my elbows, or tear my arms out of their sockets. Never had I experienced such helplessness, such inadequacy of human strength against the aroused elements. . . .

Then the raft came down again—at first gradually, for the wind was holding her, then with a shock that threatened to dismember her. Within what seemed to be but a few minutes, she then began to list to port, to the other side, just when I thought I would be safe there. It struck me in my own fear as the final effort of the raft to escape the horrible pounding. I was now hanging on to a rope with one foot on the edge of the raft and as trapped as I had been on the other side. But again she dropped back, and the deck lay level. Then, perhaps a minute or two later, I saw the water streaming past and, staring at it for a few moments unbelieving, realized that she had slid off the rock on the portside and that we were sailing. The jib, standing full in the gale, had pushed her back on an even keel, and the seas had washed her off the rock.

I sailed close to the wind to get away from the island (I later found it was one of the Brook Islands) and after a while noticed that the raft didn't obey the wheel. My flashlight lighting up my wake told me the story—the chain connecting the two rudders had parted. I had to steer, or I would go back on the rocks, so, tying a line around my waist, I went overboard and connected the loose ends of the chain again, using a rope to bring them together and swallowing more water than I had on the whole voyage. While in the water, I noticed that the lower part of both rudders had been rolled up like scrolls of tissue paper. Only a titanic force could have exerted the pressure of such twisting of thick iron. . . .

The maze of small islands and rock masses, amid which I had been trapped, lay finally behind me, and I could see a larger

island to my left (Gould Island) and a smaller one (Combe Island) to the right farther away. I sailed between them. Dawn
was really on the way now. It looked like a cloudy day. After a
while I cleared the island to my left and in the distance saw a
long mountainous ridge, either another large island (Hitchin-
brook Island) or part of the mainland. Then more islands appeared to my right, in line with the first one and strung out
evenly toward the west. I thought they might be reaching all
the way to the coast, forming a barrier, and therefore steered
to the left to keep away. This group of islands, I found out later,
was the Family Group, named so by Captain Cook in 1770, the
first white man to see them.

At nine o'clock I saw, spanning the opening between the
large mountainous island to the left and the chain of smaller
ones to the right, a long, low line. That had to be Australia—it
could be nothing else. I went up the mast for a better look and,
when I came down, felt certain that I was heading straight for
the coast of the mainland of Australia. It was a level wooded
shore, a gray dismal-looking stretch, for visibility was bad, and
now and then it rained. . . .

I had taken soundings all along and saw now sailing over two
fathoms. I had come quite near. Only a few more minutes now
. . . It seemed impossible to come to an end like this, just jogging
along—after that nightmarish voyage from Apia, that terrible
last night which still had me benumbed, all that long, long
strain. . . . And now the end, my goal, this low, silent shore—
Australia . . . I set off two red flares, in case someone was on the
beach, and a few minutes later, shortly after eleven o'clock,
swung the raft into the wind, let it drift in, and dropped my
anchor. I paid out on the line until she touched the sand, then
made fast, secured the sails, and cleared up the deck. The raft
was then wallowing broadside. I put my clearance papers from
Apia, my passport, and other documents that might be helpful
for identification in a small canvas bag, also a few distress flares,
a knife, and small machete, matches, and a compass in case I
had to go through the woods. Then I jumped into the surf. The

water was up to my waist, and I had to struggle against the backwash to get ashore. At last I stood on the beach. Australia —after 204 days in all, and eleven thousand miles! In that moment all Australia contracted into the tiny spot upon which I stood. I wanted to kneel down and embrace the wet sand. Yes, I had made it—the world's largest ocean lay behind me. The date was September 9, 1964. My exact geographical position was: 18 degrees 0.25 minutes south 146 degrees 01.5 minutes east.

I turned left toward the point I had steered for, hoping to find people, and began walking along the narrow beach. Occasionally I looked back at my raft rolling in the surf, the distress flag fluttering big in the wind. It was still raining and the clouds drifting low and gray.

Now and then I had to jump up on the bank, when a larger sea came roaring up or a fallen giant blocked my way with roots or limbs. After walking about a mile, I came to the point and saw, beyond, a lagoon or bay fringed with dense mangrove thickets. At its farther end a creek (Murray River) came into it. Could I walk around it? It didn't look promising, but I went into the woods a little way till I struck mangroves and saw the creek running back into the country, then knew that it was useless to go on and turned back to try the northern point of the beach.

When I came to my ceaselessly rolling raft, I climbed on board, checked the anchor rope, and then went back ashore. The woods looked the same here but the trees were somewhat higher. The big eucalypti looked weird and beautiful and as if belonging to a world I had not known, with their twisted smooth calico trunks from which the red or silvery bark hung down in long mournful tatters. A few times I left the beach and went into the woods, thinking I might find a road or trail, but each time was stopped by swamps and a thick green vine that made walking almost impossible. Once I heard what I thought was the whistle or call of a man but, after answering it a few times, discovered that it came from a bird.

I had walked about a mile when I came upon a large gray

steer feeding in the bushes. He didn't see me but, after I had passed, got my wind and, tossing up his head while giving me a quick look, ambled away. A little later I saw what looked like a small kangaroo sitting like a statue in an open patch and watching me. When I came nearer, it hopped into the thicket.

I was now close to the point I was aiming for, which ran out from the beach in a little spur of sand. A low dune lay in front of it, and walking on I saw above it the roofs of a few houses. Now I'll find people, I thought, but, when I stood on top of the dune, discovered that a little bay separated me from the houses. The bay, like the one on the other point, was solidly lined with mangrove thickets. Seeing no people on the other side whom I might signal to, I decided to walk around the bay and went into the woods, which consisted here mostly of high bushes and open patches of sand. Among the bushes were the tracks of what I thought were large dogs and the sharp hoof marks of wild pigs. After I had covered about a quarter of a mile, I struggled through the mangroves to the bay, to check where I was going, and saw that it was hopeless to continue, for a little further up, a creek (Tully River) barred my way. I then turned back to the point on the beach from where I had seen the houses, having decided to swim across the mouth of the bay. The sun was within an hour of going down, and I wanted to get to people so that the news of my landing would reach Teddy as quickly as possible.

I stood on the beach and was about to take off my clothes when I saw a man and woman walking on the sand on the other side, their backs turned to me. I shouted, but they seemed not to hear and, opening my bag, I took out a distress flare and sent it up. The couple now stopped and saw me, and I shouted that I wanted someone to come over with a boat. "I'll come right over," the man answered, and the two walked quickly away and disappeared in a stand of trees, and shortly afterwards the roar of an engine shattered the stillness as a speedboat came racing across the bay to me. The man and woman were in it. They

drove the boat up on the sand, and we met. They were somewhat taken aback when they saw a gaunt, old and sea-stained
man with a beard down to his chest and rolled-up dungarees.
"I'm Willis from New York," I said and stuck out my hand. The
man was Hank Penning from the nearby little town of Tully.
The lady was his wife.

They took me across the bay, and after an hour's ride in their
car, I was sitting in the little office of the local police station, and
they were checking my passport, clearance papers, and everything I had. No one up here, it seemed, had ever heard of me.
After everything had been checked and copied, and I had tied
up my papers again, another man came in and, looking suspi-
ciously at me, asked me to show my papers again. He scruti-
nized everything most carefully and took notes, then went out
on the porch, where he remained standing in the shadows and
watching me.

After a while someone came in from the porch and told me
the other man didn't believe a word of what I had said but was
certain I was an escaped convict from faraway Norfolk Island.

"Norfolk Island," I said. "That used to be a convict settlement
if I remember right, isn't it?"

"Yes," the other smiled. "It was closed down around 1850."

"Holy smoke!" I exclaimed. "Over a century ago. . . . Do I look
that old? I've been through hell and back all right but didn't
know it took that much out of me. Say, that would make me the
oldest man in Australia."

We both laughed, but I thought I would take a look at myself
as soon as I got to a mirror.

A few minutes later the telephone rang. It was Sydney—
someone had notified the wire services, and they wanted to talk
to me. Now I knew it was merely a matter of seconds before
Teddy would find out that I had landed.

Soon the big heart of Australia opened wide in welcome.
From every house in its cities, from every hut in the backbush,
rang out the cheers. The land of the brave Down Under loved

the sea and the men who went out to face it. Teddy flew out to meet me, and we spent wonderful hours walking and driving through forests and hills, through all the colored magic of a different world. Of course I had not forgotten to deliver the bag of special mail which I had carried from Apia.

The Australian Government—through the good will of Harold Holt, Minister of Finance, now Prime Minister of Australia, a lover of the sea and its dangers with whom I became acquainted over the telephone—ordered the raft brought from the desolate Queensland beach where I had landed to Sydney on board the M.S. *Boonaroo.* For carrying the raft back to New York on the S.S. *Pioneer Gem* I am indebted to Joseph Curran, President of the National Maritime Union of America and to the United States Lines, and to the Farrell Lines for taking it to Neport News, Virginia, where it will remain in the Mariners' Museum.

ENVOI

Why did I make this voyage? Dig deep enough, and you will find that it has been your dream also—even if you have never been to sea or your fathers before you. Sometime, perhaps long ages ago, they had this same dream, and it is still in your flesh and will always be—be you seventy or a hundred or a boy of twelve, for dreams never die.

But perhaps this explanation sounds too distant and too mystical to describe my urge for the solitude of the sea and unbroken horizons, and I will try to come a little closer to the subject: Ever since I was a child at my mother's knee, I heard her speak of the beauty of open fields and woods and the wise and endless sea. Truly a dreamer and seer she was, for then she had only known the sea from pictures. And so I am just walking her way.

Epilogue

William Willis was to make three more attempts at solo ocean crossings, each time from the United States to England. In June 1966 he left Montauk Point in the 11 ½-foot sailboat Little One. *He was picked up on September 27 by a Polish fishing boat 2000 miles off Montauk Point, in a trance and without food. He was to try again in 1967 and was again forced to abandon the solo voyage. In May 1968 he made his third attempt in* Little One. *A Soviet fishing vessel picked up Willis's battered boat 400 miles west of Iceland, but Willis was not on board.*

SOVIET CAPTAIN REPORTS
EVIDENCE OF WILLIS DEATH

Moscow, Dept. 29 (AP)—The captain of a Soviet fishing boat disclosed new evidence today that William Willis, the 75-year-old lone sailor from Long Island, was lost at sea in July.

"I believe that Willis is dead," *Tass*, the Soviet press agency, quoted the captain, Vladimir Ulasevich, as having reported from his trawler in the Atlantic.

The trawler discovered Mr. Willis' battered yacht adrift about 330 miles west of Ireland Sept. 20.

The mast was broken and no one was aboard.

Mr. Willis' passport, diary and some letters were found, the captain reported.

"The tragedy must have taken place on July 20 or 21," he said. The last date crossed off the calendar was July 20.

ALONE AGAINST THE ARCTIC

Colin Irwin

In 1971 a tall, 24-year-old, egret-thin Englishman Colin Irwin reached the halfway point in his attempt to navigate the entire Northwest Passage alone under sail—a feat which had never been done before.

The passage proper runs through the Bering Strait, which separates Alaska from the U.S.S.R., then plunges east through the icefields of the Beaufort Sea and, farther along, a maze of desolate, windswept islands. The eastern mouth of the passage is in Baffin Bay, off the west coast of Greenland. From there Irwin planned to sail his boat *Endeavour* home to England, across the Atlantic.

Irwin wintered in the Arctic for an eight-month siege of waiting. In July the ice would begin to break up, and if the summer was a good one, the 3000-mile passage would become navigable in August. But by mid-September it would start to freeze again.

Norway's Roald Amundsen first sailed the passage. It took him three years (1903–1906), with a three-man crew and a 47-ton sloop, with gasoline engine. Irwin's boat, *Endeavour*, had no engine. It weighed only 2500 pounds, was 18 feet long and, with its retractable keel pulled up, floated in only one foot of water. It was completely enclosed with a humped-back deck covering a tiny cabin. Irwin sailed his boat standing in a hip-wide circular hatch at the stern. The junk-style rigging and sail allowed him to sail *Endeavour* "in reverse" if she became trapped in the ice.

The ice broke up late in Southern Alaska last year. I was going to leave from Anchorage, but when *Endeavour* arrived there by rail early in June the ice was still heavy around the Aleutian Islands. Weather, as they say, is made in the Aleutians and it is bad even at the best of times. Thick fogs and heavy seas are common, the coastline is an intricate maze of inlets and islands, and with ice complicating the problems, I didn't feel like taking the risk of starting off and immediately coming to grief. So *Endeavour* was shipped to the railhead at Nenana on the Yukon River and then barged down to Galena, about 600 miles from the river mouth, which is well north of the Aleutians in the Bering Sea.

British petroleum workers and the USAF airmen at Galena gave me a big send-off and then I was alone, sailing down the muddy, mile-wide Yukon on a cloudy day.

I felt very depressed for those first few hours. The thousands of miles ahead of me seemed overwhelming and I wondered whether I hadn't really overestimated myself. I wished then someone were with me. Fortunately, there wasn't too much time to think. I had hoped to drift down into the delta, but *Endeavour* had too much windage and kept heading for one bank or the other, so I had to sail her, which was hard work. The days were long and warm, however, and the land was richly green and very beautiful.

It took my 12 days to reach the delta. The trees and hills eventually gave way to flat, open country and at the river's mouth, I guided *Endeavour* across ten miles of mud flats with the centerboard raised—because I'd lost the unmarked channel and there was only 18 inches of water. A light wind carried me across Norton Sound to Nome in four days. During the afternoons I'd sometimes lie out on deck with my shirt off.

As I left Nome and sailed into the Bering Strait, the weather began to change. There was still no ice, but the winds were fresh and the seas ran high. At the entrance to the Strait, I put in at Tin City, a USAF radar station, and set up a radio schedule so that from then on I would be in daily contact.

The wind blew from the south, pushing *Endeavour* north through the Strait in a rough sea. Siberia was a misty coastline off to port. That night, July 6, I anchored off Sheshmereff, 20 miles south of the Arctic Circle. Some Eskimos came out to *Endeavour* and took me in for a meal of frozen fish and reindeer meat.

Fragments of the Polar ice pack were reported in the area, so I hugged the coastline as I moved north, afraid of getting trapped by the large floes which drift in deep water. It grew progressively colder and the weather stayed rough. By the time I reached Point Hope it was blowing a gale. I put into the harbor for shelter, but that night *Endeavour* dragged her anchor and was driven onto the beach. There was nothing to do but abandon her in the breakers until the wind died. I put up a notice in the store the next morning, asking for help. That afternoon about a dozen men from the village came down to the boat. They brought a block and tackle and simply winched *Endeavour* up onto the beach the same way they do the whales they hunt from small boats every spring. I spent several days repairing the damage and waiting for better weather.

When the wind died I put to sea once more, only to run into new problems. First there was fog, rolling in at dusk with the cold air blowing off the Polar ice pack which I knew lay in wait over the northern horizon. It cut visibility to a few feet, it was miserably damp and cold and the feeling of isolation it gave was intensified by the utter silence. For hours all I heard was the monotonous lapping of water against *Endeavour*'s hull.

It was sometime after this, again in heavy fog, that I first met the ice. I was listening to the blast-off of Apollo XV. As Houston went into the final countdown, a towering, ghost-like mountain of ice floated sullenly out of the fog toward me. It loomed above *Endeavour*'s 20-foot mast. To counter the shock it gave me I sailed toward it for a closer look and then steered closer to shore. I had been tacking up an imaginary channel between the ten- and 30-fathom marks, using my echo sounder, but now I stayed between the three- and 20-fathom marks, guessing the ice was mostly outside that range.

But even in shallower water I began sighting floes more and more frequently. They were not icebergs—icebergs are splinters of glacial ice found only in the Atlantic—but fragments of sea ice broken off the Polar ice cap. They ranged from tiny scraps to islands hundreds of feet long, and their colors ran from emerald green to light blue. In the fog I usually heard the slap of the swell against their sides long before I could see them. The farther north I went the more of a menace they became. I could no longer set *Endeavour*'s self-starting gear and sleep as she sailed, but had to stay up, constantly on the lookout. About midday on July 26, the fog lifted to reveal the Polar ice cap itself, a thin white line that stretched across the horizon, lightening the blue sky above it to a pearl gray. The presence of the pack only drove me harder. If the wind shifted I knew it would drift in and trap me against the shore in a matter of hours. I sailed on with only one thought—to reach the shelter of the harbor at Barrow, still 200 miles away, and sleep for 24 hours. I had slept only five hours in the last 72 and began to see spots in front of my eyes. Several times I fell asleep at the helm.

It took me three more days to reach Barrow, tacking endlessly between the ice floes near the shore and fighting to stay awake. I anchored once under Skull Cliff and tried to get some sleep, but the wind came around, blowing onshore and kicking up a healthy swell. I lay awake for two hours listening to the ice floes crash into one another, waiting for one to find *Endeavour*, and then gave up and pushed on.

I reached Barrow on July 29 at 10 A.M. and there the worst news of all awaited me—the wind had shifted and the polar pack was closing in. Some Eskimos brought me ashore, but the locals told me that the pack would blockade the harbor within five hours. Bitterly dejected and fighting the urge to give up, I went back out to *Endeavour* and tacked out of the harbor and around Barrow Point into safe water. The prospect of another night on the boat was more than I could stand, so I tacked across the bay, reaching an Eskimo camp at ten o'clock that night.

The next 30 days were spent playing a frustrating game with the constantly shifting Polar ice. The moment it retreated, opening up a lead along the shoreline, I would sail east for as long as I dared, scurrying into lagoons for safety as the ice closed in again. My only advantages were the ice and weather reports broadcast daily from the Distant Early Warning (DEW Line) radar stations along the Alaskan North Slope and across Canada.

I was pinned down for five days at Flaxman Island. A narrow lead finally opened up and I tried to reach Barter Island, 50 miles across Camden Bay, tacking all night between the loose floes. By 10 A.M. I was within ten miles of the harbor, but the closer I got the more dense was the ice. In desperation I went out beyond the ten-fathom mark, where giant floes hundreds of yards long and 20 feet high had run aground, forming a honeycomb of backwaters. At dusk I was still four miles out, and then the fog rolled in and I was completely lost out in the pack. I felt certain *Endeavour* would be icebound by morning. It might be days before the pack opened up again so I radioed my position to the men at the DEW Line station on Barter Island. They passed word along to the Eskimos in the village of Kaktouik. Within two hours the Eskimos had reached me, dragging their small boats across the floes. Together we pulled *Endeavour* into the safety of the lagoon, working late into the evening, pulling, pushing and winching *Endeavour* from one lead to another until she was clear.

Again, I was pinned down at Barter Island for several days, high winds keeping the ice on shore. It was incredibly frustrating. I was only 100 miles from Herschel Island, beyond which I knew the ice would rapidly begin thinning out. I moved *Endeavour* up to the east end of the bay, close to the pack, and watched and waited. The hours dragged. The summer sun was dying fast. Snow flurries came more often now. It began to look as though I would be forced to winter here at Barter, far short of my planned stopping point at Cambridge Bay. If I had to start from here next July, my chances of completing the voyage in two summers would be slim.

At last the wind dropped and a slender shore lead opened up. It carried me down to Demarcation Bay before the pack closed in again. There was another long wait at Demarcation before the pack loosened its grip again on August 27th. The wind turned very light, from the northeast, and I tacked off the beach at noon sailing into the wind. As I sailed farther out the ice became more scattered.

At 7:30 that night I tied up to a large floe, 15 feet high and solidly aground in 60 feet of water. Since noon I had come only three miles east.

I climbed to the top of the floe, using an ice ax, to take a look around and conquer a peak no one else was likely to climb, then reboarded *Endeavour* and went below to write my log. I had just finished when a sudden swell hit the boat and I dived for the hatch as the floe I was moored to lurched, adjusting its trim. It had just shed a large chunk of itself, that was now drifting off on its own. Floes and icebergs often capsize as their center of gravity shifts, and with visions of *Endeavour* being suddenly upended I jumped ashore in my stocking feet and cast off.

I found another floe nearby that looked flat and trustworthy, tied up alongside and zipped myself into my sleeping bag. But all night long the boat clunked against the ice and I was haunted by the thought of another floe grinding into us.

The morning was shrouded in heavy mist and there was little wind. I tacked on until the wind died completely. Around two or three in the afternoon the mist lifted and there was the treeless Alaskan coastline. I took a fix on a mountain and found that *Endeavour* had been drifting west with the floes and that I'd lost 20 miles in the course of the night.

I spent another sleepless night being bumped around by oncoming ice. At dawn the wind began blowing from the west and by nine o'clock I had made up the ground lost in the last couple of days. That evening I was off Komakuch Beach and becalmed again. At noon the next day I put out for Herschel Island. The ice report was not good and neither was the weather forecast. I moved up a lead to the north-northeast for about eight miles and then the wind came up, blowing between 20 and 30 knots. It kept the bulk of the pack to starboard. But then a second pack appeared to port and for several hours I tacked about in rough seas trying to find a way through this mass of grinding, colliding ice. Herschel Island was clearly visible only 15 miles away. Beyond it the water was reported ice-free, but I could find no way through and no way back. In desperation I called a DEW Line station and was advised to try skirting the pack to the north. It worked. A few miles farther out I got into clearer water.

It was getting dark as I ran down on Herschel Island and she often fell out of view in mist. Normally I would have given her a wide berth, but the lead I was sailing in was narrow, forcing me in to the shore in total darkness. I don't believe in God, but I prayed—as most people do, I think, in a really tight spot. When the mist lifted, Herschel was a couple of miles to the southeast and what floes there were glinted white in the starlight. As I moved farther away from the island, I saw the northern lights for the first time, dancing and shimmering in whirlpools of iridescent amber above my head. Much later on I heard that eight hours after I left Komakuch Beach the ice closed in and packed hard for the winter.

From Herschel Island on, it was very cold and snow flurries often cut visibility to less than half a mile. But it was an indescribable pleasure to be moving across open water again, without the white glint of pack ice on the horizon. I was too close to the coastline to get any proper sleep, so I catnapped at the helm for a couple of days and then landed at Tuck in the MacKenzie Delta.

The day after I left Tuck, *Endeavour* covered 100 miles in 24 hours, but then the wind shifted again and I spent two days getting nowhere. The "September gales" were blowing regularly now. The channels between the islands in Coronation Gulf were narrow and what navigation aids there were had been shut down or removed for the winter and I had to sail between them in the dark and mist on dead reckoning. But nothing went wrong until I missed a tack in the lee off Cape Alexander. There wasn't room to correct my mistake and *Endeavour* was blown ashore on the windward side of a small island. I tried pushing off with an oar, but the waves were breaking against the boat too strongly. I took off my boots and trousers and went over the side to try to push her around the point into the lee of the island. She wouldn't budge. I climbed back aboard and went below, numb with cold and fumbling to light a cigarette. I was furious with myself. If I got stuck here I would have to be rescued, which would not be easy. It had taken a village of willing hands to get *Endeavour* off the beach at Point Hope and here I was a good 30 miles from Cambridge Bay—the closest settlement and the place I had picked to winter. A call for help would not be the best introduction. But I had still one hope. My charts showed that there was a couple of feet of tide here, so I put on my wet suit, went back into the water, laid an anchor out toward the shoal and winched *Endeavour*'s bow up into the waves. The anchor dragged and I had to lay it off again, making sure it was wedged in some rock. I got *Endeavour* pointing bow out again, and waited for the tide. As it came in I gradually pulled her off, but I still had to get around the point. Another error would put her aground again, so I went over the side once more, put the anchor around my neck, and, taking *Endeavour* on a short leash, walked her around the point until the wind took her clear and I was out of my depth. I dropped the anchor and scrambled aboard. Even that was difficult—spray from the breakers had coated the hull with ice.

It was now 11:30, too late to reach Cambridge Bay in daylight. I took off my wet suit and climbed into my sleeping bag. After two hours only my feet were still numb. I heated water and soaked them. For 15 minutes the pain was severe and I chain-smoked. Finally my feet turned pink, with only a few small dark patches of frostbite on the skin. I climbed back into the sleeping bag. The wind was freshening out of the northwest now and it began to snow.

At first light I sailed around the Cape and on up the coast, making radio contact with Cambridge. A small flotilla of Eskimo boats came out from the dock to meet me. They insisted on taking *Endeavour* in tow, although I wanted to sail her in myself. Only one other sailing vessel had come this far—H.M.S. *Enterprise*. *Enterprise* had sailed into Cambridge Bay late in the fall of 1852, 119 years ago, searching for Sir John Franklin's party of 129 which had vanished in the area without a trace seven years earlier. She had wintered in the bay, but then turned back towards the Bering Strait when the ice broke up the following summer.

Endeavour and I shall winter here, too, but with the thaw we will sail on and try to make it the rest of the way. The most difficult miles, through the Franklin Strait (where Franklin's ships were crushed in the ice) and Barrow Strait, lie ahead.

I can only hope that the coming summer will be a good one. If I can get through the rest of the passage at all, I'd like to get through quickly. An Atlantic crossing in late winter might well be more than even *Endeavour* can handle.

Epilogue

He has temporarily given up the idea of completing the Northwest Passage and gone off on a 500-mile solo trek across the Arctic waste using a dog sled instead of sails.

2

THE SKY

FIRST POWER FLIGHT AT KITTY HAWK

Fred Kelly

On December 17, 1903, at Kitty Hawk, North Carolina, man finally became airborne via a four-cylinder engine of 12 horsepower. The first heavier-than-air machine's entry into the sky lasted 12 seconds and went 120 feet. The fourth flight lasted 59 seconds and went 852 feet. The combined weight of the machine and the pilot, Wilbur Wright, was 750 pounds. After that, the sky and the moon were man's destinations.

It was hoped to have the power machine ready for its first trial early in November. But at the first run of the motor on the completed machine, an unexpected strain from back-firing twisted one of the propeller shafts and tore loose the cross-arm to which the propeller was fastened. Both shafts were then sent back to the bicycle shop at Dayton to be made stronger. Dr. Spratt had arrived on October 23 to witness tests of the new machine, but the weather had become so wintry that he started home on November 5, taking with him as far as Norfolk the shafts for shipment to Dayton.

Octave Chanute came, on invitation, the next day, but he too found it difficult to be comfortable with the weather increasingly wintry and he stayed less than a week. Before leaving camp, Chanute had unintentionally given them something else to worry about. He had remarked that at least twenty per cent usually must be allowed in chain transmission for loss in power. As the Wrights had allowed only five per cent, they felt considerable alarm.

Since Chanute was a capable and famous engineer, it seemed prudent to find out whose estimates were more nearly correct. After Chanute had gone, the brothers suspended one of the drive chains over a sprocket and hung a bag of sand at each end of the chain. By measuring the amount of weight on one side needed to lift that on the other, they calculated the loss in transmission. As nearly as they could tell, this loss was even less than the five per cent they had estimated.

The shafts, made of larger and heavier tubing, arrived from Dayton on November 20. When they were tested again, a new difficulty appeared. The sprockets, which were screwed to the shafts and locked with nuts of opposite thread, kept coming loose. This was a small problem, and yet the brothers did not at once see any way to solve it. They went to bed discouraged. The next day, however, they tried, as they often did, something they had learned in the bicycle business. They had found a great variety of uses for the kind of cement intended for fastening tires to rims. Once they had used it successfully in fastening the hands of a stop-watch that several watchsmiths had said was beyond repair. Why not try tire cement on those sprockets? They heated the propeller shafts and sprockets, poured melted cement into the threads and screwed them together. There were no more loose sprockets.

Just as the machine was ready for test, bad weather set in. There was rain or snow for several days and a wind of twenty-five to thirty miles an hour from the north. But while being delayed by the weather the Wrights were not idle. They busied themselves contriving a mechanism to measure automatically the duration of a flight from the time the machine started to move forward to the time it stopped, the distance traveled through the air in that time, and the number of revolutions made by the motor and propeller. A stop-watch took the time; an anemometer measured the air traveled through; and a counter took the number of revolutions made by the motor. The watch, anemometer, and revolution counter were all automatically started and stopped simultaneously.

During this time, the Wrights occupied themselves also in making tests of the strength of the wings, as well as many satisfactory tests of the engine. During a test of the engine, on November 28, they discovered that one of the recently strengthened tubular shafts had developed a flaw and cracked!

With winter almost upon them, there was no time to trust to express service in getting the shafts to Dayton. Orville decided he would go there at once. Instead of tubular shafts, they would use solid tool steel, necessary, it seemed, to take up the shock of premature or missed explosions of the engine.

Not until Friday, December 11, did Orville get back to camp. (En route, he had read in a newspaper of the last unsuccessful attempt to fly the Langley machine over the Potomac at Washington.)

It didn't take long to install the new propeller shafts and the next afternoon, Saturday, the machine was again ready for trial. But the wind was so light that a start could not have been made from the level ground with a run of only sixty feet permitted by the monorail track to be used. Nor was there enough time before dark to take the machine to one of the near-by hills, where, by placing the track on the steep incline, enough speed could be promptly attained for starting in calm air.

All day Sunday the Wrights just sat at the camp and read, hoping for suitable weather the next day. They were now particularly eager to avoid delay because of their boyish craving to be at home by Christmas. If there should be a spell of bad wintry weather they might have to stay at Kitty Hawk for another two or three weeks.

Monday, December 14, dawned beautifully clear, but cold,

and there was not enough wind to permit a start from level ground near the camp. The Wrights therefore decided to attempt a flight from the side of Kill Devil Hill. With a relatively light wind it should be all the easier to handle the machine. The pilot, whichever one of them it should be, ought to be able not only to fly successfully but to go on down far beyond the Kitty Hawk life-saving station, nearly five miles away, before landing.

Contrary to reports of secretiveness, the Wrights, naturally desiring witnesses, had extended a general invitation to people living within five or six miles to come and see their first attempt at flight. But it was impossible for them to send word or give a signal as to the exact time the attempt would be made. They had arranged, however, to put a signal on one of the sheds that could be seen from the Kill Devil Life-Saving Station only a little more than a mile away. Members of the life-saving crew were on the lookout for the signal. Soon after the signal was hung against the wall of the shed, the Wrights were joined by John T. Daniels, Robert Westcott, Thomas Beacham, W.S. Dough, and "Uncle Benny" O'Neal. All helped to get the machine to the place selected, a quarter of a mile away, on the hillside. It would not have been easy to drag the machine that distance and the Wrights used a characteristic bit of ingenuity. They set the machine on the monorail track they were going to use for the takeoff, slid it along to the end of the sixty-foot wooden rail, then took up a rear section of the track and added it to the front end. By thus re-laying the track over and over, they were able to have the machine run on wheels all the way. The sled-like skids that were the landing gear of the machine rested on a truck—a plank about six feet long, laid across a much smaller piece of wood to which were attached two small wheels, one in front of the other. Each was kept on the track by two vertical guides. These little wheels had ball-bearings. They were modified hubs from wheels of a bicycle. The rail itself was two by four inches, set on edge, with the upper surface covered by a thin strip of metal.

As soon as they reached the hill, the Wrights prepared for the test. Each was eager for the chance to make the first trial, and they tossed a coin to determine which of them it should be. Wilbur won the toss.

After the machine had been fastened to the track by wire to prevent its moving until released by the operator, one of the Wrights started the motor and let it run for a few minutes to make sure it was working properly. Then Wilbur took his place on the machine. Two small boys, with a dog, who had come to see what was going on, were scared away by the noise of the motor.

Here is Orville Wright's own account of what then happened:

I took a position at one of the wings, intending to help balance the machine as it ran down the track. But when the restraining wire was slipped, the machine started off so quickly I could stay with it only a few feet. After a 35- to 40-foot run, it lifted from the rail.

But it was allowed to turn up too much. It climbed a few feet, stalled, and then settled to the ground near the foot of the hill, 105 feet below. My stop-watch showed that it had been in the air just 3½ seconds. In landing, the left wing touched first. The machine swung around, dug the skids into the sand and broke one of them. Several other parts were also broken, but the damage to the machine was not serious. While the tests had shown nothing as to whether the power of the motor was sufficient to keep the machine up, since the landing was made many feet below the starting point, the experiment had demonstrated that the method adopted for launching the machine was a safe and practical one. On the whole, we were much pleased.

Two days were consumed in making repairs, and the machine was not ready again till late in the afternoon of the 16th. While we had it out on the track in front of the building, making the final adjustments, a stranger came along. After looking at the machine a few seconds he inquired what it was. When we told him it was a flying machine, he asked whether we intended to fly it. We said we did, as soon as we had a suitable wind. He looked at it several minutes longer and then, wishing to be courteous, remarked that it looked as if it would fly, if it had a "suitable wind." We were much amused, for, no doubt, he had in mind the recent 75-mile gale when he repeated our words, "a suitable wind!"

During the night of December 16th a strong cold wind blew from the north. When we arose on the morning of the 17th, the puddles of water, which had been standing about the camp since the recent rains, were covered with ice. The wind had a velocity of 10 to 12 meters per second (22 to 27 miles an hour). We thought it would die down before long, and so remained indoors the early part of the morning. But when ten o'clock arrived, and the wind was as brisk as ever, we decided that we had better get the machine out and attempt a flight. We hung out the signal for the men of the Life-Saving Station. We thought that by facing the flyer into a strong wind, there ought to be no trouble in launching it from the level ground about camp. We realized the difficulties of flying in so high a wind, but estimated that the added dangers in flight would be partly compensated for by the slower speed in landing.

We laid the track on a smooth stretch of ground about one hundred feet west of the new building. The biting cold wind made work difficult, and we had to warm up frequently in our living room, where we had a good fire in an improvised stove made of a large carbide can. By the time all was ready, J.T. Daniels, W.S. Dough and A.D. Etheridge, and Johnny Moore, a boy from Nag's Head, had arrived.

We had a "Richard" hand anemometer with which we measured the velocity of the wind. Measurements made just before starting the first flight showed velocities of 11 to 12 meters per second, or 24 to 27 miles per hour. Measurements made just before the last flight gave between 9 and 10 meters per second. One made just afterward showed a little over 8 meters. The records of the Government Weather Bureau at Kitty Hawk gave the velocity of the wind between the hours of 10:30 and 12 o'clock, the time during which the four flights were made, as averaging 27 miles at the time of the first flight and 24 miles at the time of the last.

With all the knowledge and skill acquired in thousands of flights in the last ten years, I would hardly think today of making my first flight on a strange machine in a twenty-seven-mile wind, even if I knew that the machine had already been flown and was safe. After these years of experience, I look with amazement upon our audacity in attempting flights with a new and untried machine under such circumstances. Yet faith in our calculations and the design of the first machine, based upon our tables of air pressures, obtained by months of careful laboratory work, and confidence in our system of control developed by three years of actual experiences in balancing gliders in the air, had convinced us that the machine was capable of lifting and maintaining itself in the air, and that, with a little practice, it could be safely flown.

Wilbur having used his turn in the unsuccessful attempt on the 14th, the right to the first trial now belonged to me. After running the motor a few minutes to heat it up, I released the wire that held the machine to the track, and the machine started forward into the wind. Wilbur ran at the side of the machine, holding the wing to balance it on the track. Unlike the start on the 14th, made in a calm, the machine, facing a 27-mile wind, started very slowly. Wilbur was able to stay with it till it lifted from the track after a forty-foot run. One of the Life-Saving men snapped the camera for us, taking a picture just as the machine had reached the end of the track and had risen to a height of about two feet. The slow forward speed of the machine over the ground is clearly shown in the picture by Wilbur's attitude. He stayed along beside the machine without any effort.

The course of the flight up and down was exceedingly erratic, partly due to the irregularity of the air and partly to lack of experience in handling this machine. The control of the front rudder was difficult on account of its being balanced too near the center. This gave it a tendency to turn itself when started, so that it turned too far on one side and then too far on the other. As a result, the machine would rise suddenly to about ten feet, and then as suddenly dart for the ground. A sudden dart when a little over a hundred feet from the end of the track, or a little over 120 feet from the point at which it rose into the air, ended the flight. As the velocity of the wind was over 35 feet per second and the speed of the machine over the ground against this wind ten feet per second, the speed of the machine relative to the air was over 45 feet per second, and the length of the flight was equivalent to a flight of 540 feet made in calm air.

This flight lasted only 12 seconds, but it was nevertheless the first in the history of the world in which a machine carrying a man had raised itself by its own power into the air in full flight, had sailed forward without reduction of speed, and had finally landed at a point as high as that from which it started.

With the assistance of our visitors we carried the machine back to the track and prepared for another flight. The wind, however, had chilled us all through, so that before attempting a second flight, we all went to the building again to warm up. Johnny Moore, seeing under the table a box filled with eggs, asked one of the Station men where we got so many of them. The people of the neighborhood eke out a bare existence by catching fish during the short fishing season, and their supplies of other articles of food are limited. He probably never had seen so many eggs at one time in his whole life.

The one addressed jokingly asked him whether he hadn't noticed the small hen running about the outside of the building. "That chicken lays eight to ten eggs a day!" Moore, having just seen a piece of machinery lift itself from the ground and fly, a thing at that time considered as impossible as perpetual motion, was ready to believe nearly anything. But after going out and having a good look at the wonderful fowl, he returned with the remark, "It's only a common-looking chicken!"

At twenty minutes after eleven Wilbur started on the second flight. The course of this flight was much like that of the first, very much up and down. The speed over the ground was somewhat faster than that of the first flight, due to the lesser wind. The duration of the flight was less than a second longer than the first, but the distance covered was about seventy-five feet greater.

Twenty minutes later, the third flight started. This one was steadier than the first one an hour before. I was proceeding along pretty well when a sudden gust from the right lifted the machine up twelve to fifteen feet and turned it up sidewise in an alarming manner. It began a lively sidling off to the left. I warped the wings to try to recover the lateral balance and at the same time pointed the machine down to reach the ground as quickly as possible. The lateral control was more effective than I had imagined and before I reached the ground the right wing was lower than the left and struck first. The time of this flight was fifteen seconds and the distance over the ground a little over 200 feet.

Wilbur started the fourth and last flight at just 12 o'clock. The first few hundred feet were up and down, as before, but by the time three hundred feet had been covered, the machine was under much better control. The course for the next four or five hundred feet had but little undulation. However, when out about eight hundred feet the machine began pitching again, and, in one of its darts downward, struck the ground. The distance over the ground was measured and found to be 852 feet; the time of the flight 59 seconds. The frame supporting the front rudder was badly broken, but the main part of the machine was not injured at all. We estimated that the machine could be put in condition for flight again in a day or two.

While we were standing about discussing this last flight, a sudden strong gust of wind struck the machine and began to turn it over. Everybody made a rush for it. Wilbur, who was at one end, seized it in front. Mr. Daniels and I, who were behind, tried to stop it by holding to the rear uprights.

All our efforts were in vain. The machine rolled over and over. Daniels, who had retained his grip, was carried along with it, and was thrown about, head over heels, inside of the machine. Fortunately he was not seriously injured, though badly bruised in falling about against the motor, chain guides, etc. The ribs in the surfaces of the machine were broken, the motor injured and the chain guides badly bent, so that all possibility of further flights with it for that year were at an end.

It is unlikely that any of the five spectators who had seen these flights sensed their scientific importance. But some of them felt interested, from one point of view, because they would have the laugh on a number of natives thereabouts who had insisted that these Wright brothers must be a pair of harmless cranks. A common argument had been: "God didn't intend man to fly. If he did, he would have given him a set of wings."

LINDBERGH'S OWN STORY

CHARLES A. LINDBERGH

Charles Augustus Lindbergh was born in 1902 in Detroit. He first studied engineering, then took up flying in 1922 and bought his first plane in 1923, to become a barnstormer and stunt flier. Commissioned a second lieutenant in the Air Force Reserve in 1925, he later flew the airmail route between Chicago and St. Louis. He flew his famous monoplane, *The Spirit of St. Louis,* in record time from San Diego to New York on May 20, 1927. On May 21 he took off on his flight to Paris.

Reprinted from The New York Times of Monday, May 23rd, 1927
Lindbergh's Own Story
of Epochal Flight
———

Tempted To Turn Back, Keeps On In Storm; Asks
Fishing Boat: 'Am I On Road To Ireland?'
———

CALLED 'LUCKY,' BUT SAYS LUCK ISN'T ALL
———

Modestly Shares Credit With Plane and Engine Builders,
Adding: 'I Hope I Made Good Use of What I Had.'
———

THE IRISH COAST WAS 'A BEAUTIFUL SIGHT' TO HIM
———

After That It Was Easy—Won't Repeat the Hazardous Trip, But
Wants "To Do a Little Flying" Over There.

———

By CAPTAIN CHARLES A. LINDBERGH

SPECIAL CABLE TO THE *NEW YORK TIMES.*

PARIS, May 22.—Well, here I am in the hands of American
Ambassador Herrick. From what I have seen of it, I am sure I
am going to like Paris.

It isn't part of my plans to fly my plane back to the United
States, although that doesn't mean I have finished my flying
career. If I thought that was going to be the result of my flight
across the Atlantic, you may be sure I would never have under-
taken it. Indeed, I hope that I will be able to do some flying over
here in Europe—that is, if the souvenir hunters left enough of
my plane last night.

Incidentally, that reception I got was the most dangerous part
of the whole flight. If wind and storm had handled me as vigor-
ously as that Reception Committee of Fifty Thousand I would
never have reached Paris and wouldn't be eating a 3-o'clock-in-
the-afternoon breakfast here in Uncle Sam's Embassy.

There's one thing I wish to get straight about this flight. They
call me "Lucky," but luck isn't enough. As a matter of fact, I had
what I regarded and still regard as the best existing plane to
make the flight from New York to Paris. I had what I regard as
the best engine, and I was equipped with what were in the
circumstances the best possible instruments for making such
efforts. I hope I made good use of what I had.

That I landed with considerable gasoline left means that I had recalled the fact that so many flights had failed because of lack of fuel, and that was one mistake I tried to avoid.

WEATHER ALMOST MADE HIM TURN BACK

All in all, I couldn't complain of the weather. It wasn't what was predicted. It was worse in some places and better in others. In fact, it was so bad once that for a moment there came over me the temptation to turn back. But then I figured it was probably just as bad behind me as in front of me, so I kept on toward Paris.

As you know, we (that's my ship and I) took off rather suddenly. We had a report somewhere around 4 o'clock in the afternoon before that the weather would be fine, so we thought we would try it.

We had been told we might expect good weather mostly during the whole of the way. But we struck fog and rain over the coast not far from the start. Actually, it was comparatively easy to get to Newfoundland, but real bad weather began just about dark, after leaving Newfoundland, and continued until about four hours after daybreak. We hadn't expected that at all, and it sort of took us by surprise, morally and physically. That was when I began to think about turning back.

IN SERIOUS DANGER FROM A SLEET STORM

Then sleet began, and, as all aviators know, in a sleet storm one may be forced down in a very few minutes. It got worse and worse. There, above and below me, and on both sides, was that driving storm. I made several detours trying to get out of it, but in vain. I flew as low as ten feet above the water and then mounted up to ten thousand feet. Along toward morning the storm eased off, and I came down to a comparatively low level.

I had seen one ship just before losing sight of Newfoundland, and I saw the glow of several others afterward through the mist and storm. During the day I saw no ships until near Ireland.

I had, as I said, no trouble before I hit the storm I referred to. We had taken off at 7:55 in the morning. The field was slightly damp and soft, so the take-off was longer than it would have been otherwise. I had no trouble getting over the houses and trees. I kept out of the way of every obstacle and was careful not to take any unnecessary chances. As soon as I cleared everything, the motor was throttled down to three-fourths and kept there during the whole flight, except when I tried to climb over the storm.

CHECKED HIS COURSE AT NEWFOUNDLAND

Soon after starting I was out of sight of land for 300 miles, from Cape Cod over the sea to Nova Scotia. The motor was acting perfectly and was carrying well the huge load of 451 gallons of gasoline and 20 gallons of oil, which gave my ship the greatest cruising radius of any plane of its type.

I passed over St. John's, N.F., purposely going out of my way a few miles to check up. I went right through the narrow pass, going down so low that it could be definitely established where I was at that hour. That was the last place I saw before taking to the open sea.

I had made preparations before I started for a forced landing if it became necessary, but after I started I never thought much about the possibility of such a landing. I was ready for it, but I saw no use thinking about it, inasmuch as one place would have been about as good or as bad as another.

Despite the talk about my periscope, I had no trouble in

regard to visibility. The view I had on both sides was quite good enough for navigating the ocean, and the purpose of the periscope was only to enable me to see any obstacle directly in front of me. The periscope was useful in starting from New York and landing in Paris. Other than that I used it very little. I kept a map in front of me and an instrument showing practically where I was all of the time

THE EIGHTH HOUR
Over Nova Scotia
Time—2:52 P.M.

Wind Velocity	15 *m.p.h.*	Visibility	*Unlimited*
Wind Direction	*SSW.*	Altitude	600 *feet*
True Course	64°	Air Speed	96 *m.p.h.*
Variation	25° *W.*	Tachometer	1650 *r.p.m.*
Magnetic Course	89°	Oil Temperature	39 *C.*
Deviation	0°	Oil Pressure	58 *lbs.*
Compass Course	89°	Fuel Pressure	3.5 *lbs.*
Drift Angle	5°*L.*	Mixture	2
Compass Heading	94°	Fuel Tank	*Fuselage*
Ceiling	*Unlimited*		

FLEW OVER AN ICEBERG ZONE

Shortly after leaving Newfoundland I began to see icebergs. There was a low fog and even through it I could make out bergs clearly. It began to get very cold, but I was well prepared for cold. I had on ordinary flying clothing, but I was down in the cockpit, which protected me, and I never suffered from the weather.

Within an hour after leaving the coast it became dark. Then I struck clouds and decided to try to get over them. For a while I succeeded, at a height of 10,000 feet. I flew at this height until early morning. The engine was working beautifully and I was not sleepy at all. I felt just as if I was driving a motorcar over a smooth road, only it was easier.

Then it began to get light and the clouds got higher. I went under some and over others. There was sleet in all of these clouds and the sleet began to cling to the plane. That worried me a great deal and I debated whether I should keep on or go back. I decided I must not think any more about going back. I realized that it was henceforth only a question of getting there. I was too far to turn back.

THE SIXTEENTH HOUR
Over the Atlantic
Time—10:52 P.M.

Wind Velocity	Unknown	Visiblity	Unlimited outside of clouds
Wind Direction	Unknown		
True Course	69°		
Variation	33° W.	Altitude	10,200 feet
Magnetic Course	102°	Air Speed	86 m.p.h.
Deviation	0°	Tachometer	1675 r.p.m.
Compass Course	102°	Oil Temperature	33°C.
Drift Angle	10°R.	Oil Pressure	60 lbs.
Compass Heading	92°	Fuel Pressure	3 lbs.
Ceiling	Unlimited above clouds	Mixture	4
		Fuel tank	Fuselage

THOUGHT OF THE AIR MAIL FLIERS BACK HOME

The engine was working perfectly and that cheered me. I was going along a hundred miles an hour and I knew that if the motor kept on turning I would get there. After that I thought only about navigating, and then I thought that I wasn't so badly off after all.

It was true that the flight was thirty-four hours long, and that at almost any moment in it a forced landing might be what you might call "rather interesting," but I remembered that the flying boys I knew back home spent some hours almost every week in bad flying when a forced landing would have been just as bad for them as a forced landing would have been for me.

Those boys don't get credit for it, that's all, and without doubt in a few years many people will be taking just as many chances as I took.

The only real danger I had was at night. In the daytime I knew where I was going, but in the evening and at night it was largely a matter of guesswork. However, my instruments were so good that I never could get more than 200 miles off my course, and that was easy to correct, and I had enough extra gasoline to take care of a number of such deviations. All in all, the trip over the Atlantic, especially the latter half, was much better than I expected.

Laymen have made a great deal of the fact that I sailed without a navigator and without the ordinary stock of navigation instruments, but my real director was my earth inductor compass. I also had a magnetic compass, but it was the inductor compass which guided me so faithfully that I hit the Irish coast only three miles from the theoretic point that I might have hit if I had had a navigator. I replaced a navigator's weight by the inductor compass. This compass behaved so admirably that I am ashamed to hear anyone talk about my luck. Maybe I am lucky, but all the same I knew at every moment where I was going.

The inductor compass is based on the principle of the relation between the earth's magnetic field and the magnetic field generated in the airplane. When the course has been set so that the needle registered zero on this compass, any deviation from any cause would cause the needle to swing away from zero in the direction of the error. By flying the plane with the needle at an equal distance on either side of zero and for about the same time the error had been committed, the plane would be back on her course again. This inductor compass was so accurate that I really needed no other guide.

"AM I ON THE RIGHT ROAD TO IRELAND?"

Fairly early in the afternoon I saw a fleet of fishing boats. On some of them I could see no one, but on one of them I saw some men and flew down, almost touching the craft and yelled at them, asking if I was on the right road to Ireland.

They just stared. Maybe they didn't hear me. Maybe I didn't hear them. Or maybe they thought I was just a crazy fool.

An hour later I saw land. I have forgotten just what time it was. It must have been shortly before 4 o'clock. It was rocky land and all my study told me it was Ireland. And it was Ireland!

I slowed down and flew low enough to study the land and be sure of where I was; and, believe me, it was a beautiful sight. It was the most wonderful looking piece of natural scenery I have ever beheld.

After I had made up my mind that it was Ireland, the right place for me to strike rather than Spain or some other country, the rest was child's play. I had my course all marked out carefully from approximately the place where I hit the coast, and you know it is quite easy to fly over strange territory if you have good maps and your course prepared.

FLEW LOW OVER IRELAND SO HE COULD BE SEEN

I flew quite low enough over Ireland to be seen, but apparently no great attention was paid to me. I also flew low over England, mounted a little over the Channel and then came down close to land when I passed a little west of Cherbourg. From Cherbourg I headed for the Seine and followed it upstream.

THE THIRTY-THIRD HOUR
Over France
Hours of Fuel Consumed
Nose Tank
¼ + ᴌᴴᵀ 111

Left Wing	Center Wing	Right Wing
¼ + 111	¼ +	¼ + 111

Fuselage
ᴌᴴᵀ ᴌᴴᵀ ᴌᴴᵀ 11

I noticed it gets dark much later over here than in New York and I was thankful for that. What especially pleased me was the ease with which I followed my course after hitting the coast of Ireland.

When I was about half an hour away from Paris I began to see rockets and Very lights sent up from the air field, and I knew I was all right.

EIFFEL TOWER LIGHTS COME INTO VIEW

I saw an immense vertical electric sign, which I made out to be the Eiffel Tower. I circled Paris once and immediately saw Le Bourget [the aviation field], although I didn't know at first what it was. I saw a lot of lights, but in the dark I couldn't make out any hangars. I sent Morse signals as I flew over the field, but no one appears to have seen them. The only mistake in all my calculations was that I thought Le Bourget was northeast rather than east of Paris.

Fearing for a moment that the field I had seen—remember I couldn't see the crowd—was some other airfield than Le Bourget, I flew back over Paris to the northwest, looking for Le Bourget. I was slightly confused by the fact that whereas in America when a ship is to land, beacons are put out when floodlights are turned on, at Le Bourget both beacons and floodlights were going at the same time.

I was anxious to land where I was being awaited. So when I didn't find another airfield, I flew back toward the first lights I had seen, and flying low I saw the light of numberless automobiles. I decided that was the right place, and I landed.

RECEPTION THE MOST DANGEROUS PART OF TRIP

I appreciated the reception which had been prepared for me, and had intended taxiing up to the front of the hangars, but no sooner had my plane touched ground than a human sea swept toward it. I saw there was danger of killing people with my propeller, and I quickly came to a stop.

That reception was the most dangerous part of the trip. Never in my life have I seen anything like that human sea. It isn't clear to me yet just what happened. Before I knew it I had been hoisted out of the cockpit, and one moment was on the shoulders of some men and the next moment on the ground.

It seemed to be even more dangerous for my plane than for me. I saw one man tear away the switch and another took something out of the cockpit. Then, when they started cutting pieces of cloth from the wings. I struggled to get back to the plane, but it was impossible.

CLUBBED BY A GOOD SAMARITAN

A brave man with good intentions tried to clear a way for me with a club. Swinging the club back, he caught me on the back of the head.

It isn't true that I was exhausted. I was tired, but I wasn't exhausted.

Several French officers asked me to come away with them and I went, casting anxious glances at my ship. I haven't seen it since, but I am afraid it suffered. I would regret that very much because I want to use it again.

But I must remember that crowd did welcome me. Good Lord! There must have been a million of them. Other men will fly the Atlantic as I did, but I think it safe to guess that none of them will get any warmer reception than I got.

Finally I got here to Ambassador Herrick's house and I have certainly been all right since then.

HE DOES WANT TO DO A LITTLE FLYING!

I don't know how long I will stay in Paris. It looks like a good place. I have been asked if I intend to fly back to New York. I don't think I shall try that. But I certainly hope to get to do a little flying over here. Flying is my job and because I did this job successfully it doesn't mean I'm through.

I look forward to the day when transatlantic flying will be a regular thing. It is a question largely of money. If people can be found willing to spend enough to make proper preparations, there is no reason why it can't be made very practical. Of course, there are many things to be studied, one of the important points being whether the single-motor or multimotor ship is best. I understand there is soon to be a transatlantic flight made with a tri-motor plane. [This is evidently a reference to Commander Byrd's projected flight in the *America*.]

I didn't bring any extra clothes with me. I am wearing a borrowed suit now. It was a case of clothes or gasoline, and I took the gasoline. I have a check on a Paris bank and am going to cash it tomorrow morning, buy shirts, socks and other things.

I expect to have a good time in Paris.

But I do want to do a little flying over here.

From the New York Times of Tuesday, May 24th

Monoplane Was Best Craft For His Trip Says Lindbergh

But He Forecasts Heavy Airplanes With Multiple Motors for
Regular Service—Better Weather Reports Needed and
Water Stations Along the Route—Perfectly
'Comfortable' on Flight

By CAPTAIN CHARLES A. LINDBERGH

*Copyright 1927 in the United States, Canada, Mexico, Cuba,
South America, Europe and the British Empire by The New York
Times Company.
All Rights Reserved.
Special Cable to The New York Times.*

PARIS, May 23. —I am convinced that it is much easier to fly
from America to Europe than to fly from Europe to America.
The air drift is from west to east, and the prevailing wind, when
the weather is good, is from the southwest or northwest. If the
wind is from the east, favoring flight from Europe, then the
weather is likely to be bad.

During my flight I was helped enormously by the fact that I
had a tail wind for fully a third of the way, especially the last
part. It put me right ahead of my time schedule. I expected to
make the trip in thirty-six hours, but my actual time was thirty-
three hours and twenty minutes.

I see today that the two English fliers, Lieutenants Carr and
Gillman, on their flight to India, flew thirty-three hours and
thirty-three minutes, just a few minutes longer than I took. It
was particularly bad luck that they should have failed when so
near the end of their journey and after such a long flight. That
within the same period as I made my trip two other men with
a different machine should cover almost the same distance is
proof that there is nothing freakish about my trip. Airplanes and

men can do it, and every attempt, even though they don't all succeed, is helping aviation forward every day.

MOTOR NOT TOUCHED SINCE SAN DIEGO

Before I tried the New York–Paris flight the longest trip I had made was in bringing my ship from San Diego to St. Louis. That Wright motor I have is certainly wonderful. It hasn't been touched since I left San Diego. That is to say, it has been running sixty hours without any trouble. It has been checked, but it hasn't been touched in any way, and today when I looked at it, it seemed as sound as ever.

About my trip, there wasn't any of that casual unpreparedness which some people seem to think there was. I had everything of the very best, and every care was taken in the preparation of the trip. The actual construction of the ship was begun on the twentieth of February, and within exactly sixty days she did her first trial.

If I have been lucky, it was because I got fitted out with a perfect ship, equipped by men who took every care and precaution. Nothing was overlooked, and from the first we never had any trouble or setback. I had the pick of everything in the way of equipment.

For the flight of the kind I planned, my monoplane was undoubtedly the best ship. For regular transatlantic service, of course, something heavier, with multiple motors, will have to be developed, and I am very interested to see what will be the result of the Fokker trip with a tri-motor plane. I am sure they will get here. [Again, the allusion is to Commander Byrd's contemplated flight in the *America*.]

OCEAN STATIONS FOR COMMERCIAL FLYING

My trip was just a quick, single man's jump. Later, there will have to be developed water stations and regular ports of call, as, for instance, in South Ireland and Newfoundland, for transatlantic service. We shall have to have, too, far greater development of weather observation in the North Atlantic. Regular observation ships will have to be kept there during the flying months, sending out morning and evening reports of atmospheric conditions.

The sleet which I met with might, if it had been heavier, would have ended my trip very soon after I left Newfoundland, for it takes very little to force a plane down. If I had known I was to encounter sleet, I might never have started when I did. It was fortunate for me that I was able to rise above it most of the time, and I never was happier about anything than when the temperature rose and I got out of that danger.

To my mind, proper meteorological observation and reports about conditions over the Atlantic are the first essentials in any development of transatlantic flying. These reports can be obtained only by having regular water stations along the ocean route, with full meteorological and all other kinds of equipment, to give advice and help to airmen.

That will come, I feel sure. Though my monoplane is the first to make the trip from New York to Paris, it is going to have many successors. Regular service, however, can only be done with multimotor planes, so that if one motor stops, the plane can return. You cannot expect passengers to trust themselves to a single-motored ship.

NEVER UNCOMFORTABLE ON HIS FLIGHT

My machine, from a pilot's point of view, had the great advantage that the cabin was practically enclosed and I was well sheltered. I think that if I had been exposed to wind and sleet I would have been far more tired than I was. I see that some airmen who have looked at my ship think I must have been very uncomfortable.

Perhaps the seat looks more uncomfortable than it is. Actually, I was perfectly at my ease, except, of course, that I had to sit in the same position so long. But when one is busy with a problem and working, one never thinks much about that. I scarcely remember now if I ever thought about discomfort at all. My seat was really far more comfortable than one usually finds in a theatre or a classroom, and I didn't feel in any way cramped or strained.

With regard to eating and drinking I had fairly much the same disregard for physical sensations. I took two or three drinks of water from a big supply I had, but never much at a time. I never drink alcohol at all, and I never felt really thirsty until I landed. Then I wanted to drink a lot, and I kept on drinking milk and water all that evening after I got to the American Embassy.

Of my sandwiches I ate only one and a half, and I cannot remember now in the least what they tasted like. All airmen know quite well how indifferent one is to meal times and physical needs when one concentrates on getting anywhere. My compass kept my interest all the way. I couldn't do more than attend to it and watch the weather.

WILL LET PARISIANS "SEE US IN THE AIR"

I brought a sealed barograph with me, which will tell an interesting story of the heights at which I flew. I can see through the glass cover one very high peak where I must have gone fully 10,000 feet, though just before, I had been close down on the water. The climbing power of the plane, even while I still had a heavy load of gasoline, was one of the factors which made success possible. If my ship hadn't been able to climb as she did, the sleet would have proved far more troublesome and dangerous.

I was greatly relieved today when I went to Le Bourget, to find that less damage had been done to my ship by souvenir hunters than I had feared. There was someone with a sharp knife who now is in possession of a nice-sized square of the fuselage, and one or two other little bits of damage have been done, but it can all be repaired in an hour or two, and within the next few days I hope to be able to fly over Paris and let all the folk who have been so kind to me see us in the air.

Emergency Equipment Carried in the *Spirit of St. Louis* on the Flights Between San Diego and Paris

1	air raft, with pump and repair kit
1	canteen of water—4 quarts
1	Armbrust cup
5	cans of Army emergency rations
1	hunting knife
1	ball of cord
1	ball of string
1	large needle
1	flashlight
4	red flares, sealed in rubber tubes
1	match safe with matches
1	hack-saw blade

ACROSS THE ATLANTIC—SOLO

AMELIA EARHART

Born in Atchison, Kansas, on July 24, 1899, Amelia Earhart studied medicine at Columbia University. In 1920 she studied flying in Los Angeles, making her first solo flight after ten hours of instruction. Later she did social work in Boston, became the aviation editor of *Cosmopolitan* magazine—and started her real life as a flier. She received many awards all over the world, and her career took her everywhere as a flier. Her disappearance in 1937 in the Pacific is now legendary.

LONDON, MAY 25, 1932

Active preparation for the Atlantic Flight started after I had finished the manuscript of "The Fun Of It." Indeed, the book itself was finished by the time I left New York. . . . Here, at the request of the publishers, is a final chapter describing the flight itself——a postscript from overseas.

Starting from Harbor Grace, Newfoundland, on the afternoon of May 20, 1932, I landed near Londonderry in the north of Ireland the next morning, thirteen and a half hours after the takeoff. That, briefly, is the story of my solo flight across the Atlantic.

Ever since my first crossing in the *Friendship* in 1928 when I was merely a passenger, I have wanted to attempt a solo flight. Then, a few months ago I decided upon it seriously. My Lockheed-Vega plane, which had been under charter to a transport line at Washington, was free. I found that Bernt Balchen was ready to take charge of its re-conditioning, while my husband, always a good sport about my flying activities, was ready to back the plan with full enthusiasm. For several reasons it seemed wise not to talk about the proposed flight in advance. After all, there was nothing to talk about until it became an actuality, and from the start I definitely planned that I might abandon it at any time.

It was clear in my mind that I was undertaking the flight merely for the fun of it. I chose to fly the Atlantic because I wanted to. It was, in a measure, a self-justification—a proving to me, and to anyone else interested, that a woman with adequate experience could do it.

The plane was taken to Teterboro Airport in New Jersey just across the Hudson from New York. There is located the now unused Fokker plant, and close by lived Bernt Balchen, who with his wife are close friends of Mr. Putnam and mine. Bernt of course is one of the very finest flyers living, and also a great technician with rare engineering training. He has the happy characteristic of conservatism and being unhurried in his judgments. At the outset we told Bernt that if at any time he thought I couldn't do it, or the ship couldn't do it, I would quit, and no harm done. But Bernt never once wavered in his confidence, and that confidence helped immeasurably in sustaining my own.

First Balchen and his helpers strengthened the fuselage of the Lockheed which had had some hard knocks in the three years I have flown it. Then extra fuel tanks were put in the wings and a large tank installed in the cabin. These increased the fuel capacity to 420 gallons, giving the plane a cruising radius of about 3200 miles.* In addition, there was tankage for 20 gallons of oil. Loaded, the plane weighed about 5500 pounds.

Additional instruments were installed, including a drift indicator and additional compasses. Of the latter I had three—a periodic, magnetic and gyroscopic, each checking against the other.

From Pratt & Whitney in Hartford I secured a new "Wasp" motor, for my old one had flown a bit too long for the Atlantic grind. This was a supercharged engine developing 500 horsepower which behaved magnificently under grueling conditions. As important as the motor is its fuel and oil, and under the guidance of Major Edwin Aldrin, an accomplished flyer, my tanks were filled at Teterboro, and later at St. John and Harbor Grace, with Stanavo gasoline and oil.

During this time of preparation the plane was chartered to Bernt Balchen, who was actively working with Lincoln Ellsworth in preparation for a South Polar flight. Ellsworth was having another plane built on the Pacific Coast and it was taken for granted that Balchen was making tests with mine with the possibility of including it also in their Antarctic program. In the meanwhile, as opportunity offered, I would drive over from my home at Rye and get in odd hours in the air. Most of these were devoted to blind flying until I felt really confident of my ability to handle the ship without looking outside of the cockpit—that is, flying it solely with instruments.

As May moved on we studied the weather maps with increasing interest. As usual with all flight projects, Dr. James H. Kimball in the New York office of the United States Weather Bureau was of the greatest assistance. We never talked definitely of my plans and I don't know that he was aware exactly what was up until the last moment. He was, as always, tireless in his cooperation.

*Ed. note: On the course Miss Earhart flew, the shortest distance from Harbor Grace to the Irish coast was 1860 miles. The distance she actually flew was 2026½ miles and the distance from Harbor Grace to Paris 2640 miles.

On the afternoon of the eighteenth of May, the weather map was anything but promising. A persistent "low" with its inevitable bad weather hung over the eastern Atlantic. It seemed probable that many days might elapse before a promising break would come. Much as I wanted to move up to Harbor Grace to be ready, I was almost resigned to further days of waiting.

On Friday, the twentieth, my husband went to town and later in the morning I drove to Teterboro to talk things over with Bernt and do a little flying. The ship by then was ready to go. I arrived about 11:30. Eddie Gorski, our mechanic at the hangar, told me there was a telephone call. It was my husband, at Dr. Kimball's office. They had just gone over the morning ,weather reports, from ships at sea, from England and from the key stations of the United States.

"And how is it from here to Harbor Grace?" I asked.

"Perfect. Fine visibility all the way."

That settled it.

"We'll go this afternoon," I told my husband. "I'll see Bernt and will get off as soon as possible."

Ten minutes later, after Bernt and I had talked, I called back and told Mr. Putnam that we planned to start at three. For me there wasn't time for luncheon. Instead I drove back to Rye as fast as I could. There I changed into jodphurs and windbreaker, gathered up my leather flying suit, maps and a few odds and ends and raced back to the field.

I reached the field at 2:55 P.M. At 3:15 we took off. Three hours and forty minutes later we were at St. John, New Brunswick. Early the next morning we flew to Harbor Grace in Newfoundland arriving at 2:15 P.M. There detailed weather reports from Mr. Putnam awaited us. The outlook wasn't perfect but it was promising. I had planned to leave Harbor Grace in the evening. Thus by the time night came the load would be lightened somewhat while I would still be fresh for night flying.

Bernt had flown the plane to Harbor Grace while I rested in the fuselage behind the extra tank, with Eddie Gorski beside me. So, the start decided, I left Bernt and Eddie checking ship and motor while I found a friendly bed and restful nap. In ample time I was awakened. The later telegrams confirmed our decision. At the field, the engine was warmed up. A final message from my husband was handed to me. I shook hands with Bernt and Eddie, and climbed into the cockpit. The southwest wind was nearly right for the runway. At twelve minutes after seven, I gave her the gun. The plane gathered speed, and despite the heavy load rose easily.

A minute later I was headed out to sea.

For several hours there was fair weather with a lingering sunset. And then the moon came up over a low bank of clouds. For those first hours I was flying at about 12,000 feet. And then something happened that has never occurred in my twelve years of flying. The altimeter, the instrument which records height above ground, failed. Suddenly the hands swung around the dial uselessly and I knew the instrument was out of commission for the rest of the flight.

About 11:30, the moon disappeared behind some clouds, and I ran into rather a severe storm with lightning, and I was considerably buffeted about, and with difficulty held my course. In fact, I probably got off my course at this point to some extent because it was very rough. This lasted for at least an hour. Then I flew on in calmer weather though in the midst of clouds. Once I saw the moon for a fleeting instant and thought I could pull out on top of the clouds, so I climbed for half an hour when suddenly I realized I was picking up ice.

I knew by the climb of the ship which was not as fast as usual that it was accumulating a weight of ice. Then I saw slush on the windowpane. In addition, my tachometer, the instrument which registers revolutions per minute of the motor, picked up ice and spun around the dial.

In such a situation one has to get into warmer air, so I went down hoping the ice would melt. I descended until I could see the waves breaking although I could not tell exactly how far I was above them. I kept flying here until fog came down so low that I dared not keep on at such an altitude. Instrument-flying cannot be done safely very near the surface with the equipment we have today.

There was nothing left but to seek a middle ground, that is, to fly under the altitude at which I picked up ice and over the water by a sufficient margin. This would have been much easier to do had I been able to know my height.

Later, I tried going up again with the same result. So I gave up, just plowing through the "soup" and not looking out of the cockpit again until morning came. I depended on the instruments there to tell me the position of the plane in space, as under these conditions human faculties fail. Had I not been equipped with the best I could never have succeeded. The gyro compass, which is freest of all from fluctuations, was a real life-saver.

About four hours out of Newfoundland, I noticed that the flames were coming through a broken weld in the manifold ring. I knew that it would grow worse as the night wore on. However the metal was very heavy and I hoped it would last until I reached land. I was indeed sorry that I had looked at the break at all because the flames appeared so much worse at night than they did in the daytime.

As daylight dawned, I found myself between two layers of clouds, the first very high, probably twenty thousand feet, the lower ones little fluffy white clouds near the water. This was the first sight of the sea in daylight.

I noticed from the blowing foam that there was a northwest wind. The little white clouds soon grew packed and resembled a vast snow field. I could see on the leading edge of my wings particles of ice which had not yet melted. Soon I went a little higher and ran into another bank of clouds. I was in these for at least an hour and then came out in a clear space again over the white snow fields.

By this time, the upper layer was thin enough for the sun to come through, and it was as dazzling as on real snow. I had dark glasses but it was too much for me even so, and I came down through the lower layer to fly in the shade, as it were.

Anyway, ten hours had passed, and I wished to see the water lest I was passing a boat. I had seen one vessel shortly after I left Harbor Grace. I blinked my navigation lights but apparently no one saw me as I was flying high. Then I picked up either a fishing vessel or an oil tanker off the coast of Ireland, but those were the only two I saw until I met a fleet near the coast.

From then on I met sunshine and low hanging clouds, most of which I kept under even though they were ever near the water.

By the way, I didn't bother much about food for myself. The really important thing was fuel for the engine. It drank some 350 gallons of gasoline. My own trans-Atlantic rations consisted of one can of tomato juice which I punctured and sipped through a straw.

Of course, the last two hours were the hardest. My exhaust manifold was vibrating very badly, and then I turned on the reserve tanks and found the gauge leaking. I decided I should come down at the very nearest place, wherever it was. I had flown a set compass course all night. Now I changed to due east and decided to head for Ireland. I did not wish to miss the tip of Ireland and the weather was such I couldn't see very far. I thought I must be south of the course, for I had been told by the weather man in New York that I might find rain south of my course. There was a wind which might blow it on, so when I ran into the storm I thought that I was in this weather spoken of. Then when I saw the northwest wind, I was sure I must be south. As it happened, I probably was exactly on my course, and I think I hit Ireland about the middle.

I started down the coast and found thunderstorms lower in the hills. Not having the altimeter and not knowing the country, I was afraid to plow through these lest I hit one of the mountains, so I turned north where the weather seemed to be better and soon came across a railroad which I followed hoping it would lead me to a city, where there might be an airport.

The first place I encountered was Londonderry, and I circled it hoping to locate a landing field but found lovely pastures instead. I succeeded in frightening all the cattle in the country, I think, as I came down low several times before finally landing in a long, sloping meadow. I couldn't have asked for better landing facilities, as far as that. There ended the flight and my happy adventure. Beyond it lay further adventures of hospitality and kindness at the hands of my friends in England, France and America.

New York Times, July 13, 1967
NAVY DECLASSIFIES ITS FILES
ON AMELIA EARHART FLIGHT

WASHINGTON, July 12 (UPI)—The Navy said tonight that it had declassified several files concerning the ill-fated around-the-world flight of Amelia Earhart, the American aviatrix.

Miss Earhart, with her co-pilot, Fred J. Noonan, disappeared in 1937 between New Guinea and Howland Island in the South Pacific on the second leg of their planned flight around the world.

There has been speculation that they were either shot down or captured by the Japanese because Miss Earhart and Mr. Noonan had been working for American intelligence while on the trip.

"Nothing in our files indicates that Amelia Earhart was on a spy mission for the United States Navy," a spokeman said.

The files indicated, however, that Miss Earhart apparently ran out of gasoline northwest of Howland Island.

3

THE ANTARCTIC

ALONE

ADMIRAL RICHARD E. BYRD

Admiral Richard Evelyn Byrd, the aviator and polar explorer, made many record flights during the pioneering days of Arctic exploration, including the first flights over the North and the South poles. In 1933, when his expedition was bivouacked between Little America and the South Pole, Admiral Byrd decided to spend a scientific winter alone at the Bolling Advance Weather Base. From his book, *Alone,* I have chosen two parts—the decision to go it alone, and then the terrors and dangers in the lonely world of the Antarctic's long, wintry nights.

1933: THE IDEA

Bolling Advance Weather Base, which I manned alone during the Antarctic winter night of 1934, was planted in the dark immensity of the Ross Ice Barrier, on a line between Little America and the South Pole. It was the first inland station ever occupied in the world's southernmost continent. My decision to winter there was harder, perhaps, than even some of the men at Little America appreciated. For the original plan had been to staff the base with several men; but, as we shall presently see, this had proved impossible. In consequence, I had to choose

whether to give up the Base entirely—and the scientific mission
with it—or to man it by myself. I could not bring myself to give
it up.

This much should be understood from the beginning: that
above everything else, and beyond the solid worth of weather
and auroral observations in the hitherto unoccupied interior of
Antarctica and my interest in these studies, I really wanted to
go for the experience's sake. So the motive was in part personal.
Aside from the meteorological and auroral work, I had no important purposes. There was nothing of that sort. Nothing whatever, except one man's desire to know that kind of experience
to the full, to be by himself for a while and to taste peace and
quiet and solitude long enough to find out how good they really
are.

It was all that simple. And it is something, I believe, that
people beset by the complexities of modern life will understand
instinctively. We are caught up in the winds that blow every
which way. And in the hullabaloo the thinking man is driven to
ponder where he is being blown and to long desperately for
some quiet place where he can reason undisturbed and take
inventory. It may be that I exaggerate the need for occasional
sanctuary, but I do not think so—at least speaking for myself,
since it has always taken me longer than the average person to
think things out. By that I do not mean to imply that, before I
went to Advance Base, my private life had not been extraor-
dinarily happy; actually it had been happier than I had had right
to expect. Nevertheless, a crowding confusion had pushed in.
For fourteen years or so various expeditions, one succeeding
the other, had occupied my time and thoughts, to the exclusion
of nearly everything else. In 1919 it was the Navy's transatlantic
flight; in 1925, Greenland; in 1926, the North Pole; in 1927, the
Atlantic Ocean; 1928–30, the South Pole; and 1933–35, the
Antarctic again. In between there was no rest. An expedition
was hardly finished before I was engaged in putting a new one
together; and meanwhile I was lecturing from one end of the

country to the other in order to make a living and pay off the debts of the completed expedition, or else scurrying around to solicit money and supplies for a new one.

You might think that a man whose life carries him into remote places would have no special need for quietude. Whoever thinks that has little knowledge of expeditions. Most of the time they move in fearful congestion and uproar, and always under the lash of time. Nor will they ever be different, so long as explorers are not rich men and so long as exploration itself deals with uncertainties. No doubt the world thinks it is a fine thing to reach one pole, or both poles, for that matter. Thousands of men have devoted the best part of their lifetimes to reaching one pole or the other, and a good many have died on the way. But among the handful who have actually attained Latitude 90°, whether North or South, I doubt that even one found the sight of the pole itself particularly inspiring. For there is little enough to see: at one end of the earth a mathematical spot in the center of a vast and empty ocean, and at the other end an equally imaginary spot in the middle of a vast and windy plateau. It's not getting to the pole that counts. It's what you learn of scientific value on the way. Plus the fact that you get there and back without being killed.

Now, I had been to both poles. In prospect this had promised to be a satisfying achievement. And in a large sense it had been —principally because the poles had been the means of enabling me to enlist public support for the full-scale scientific program which was my real interest. The books of clippings which my family kept up grew fat, and most of them said good things. These were among the tangibles of success, at least in my profession; these, plus goodwill, were the visible assets, although I should point out that the wisest among us, like conservative accountants, seldom carry the latter item in excess of $1.

But for me there was little sense of true achievement. Rather, when I finished the stocktaking, I was conscious of a certain aimlessness. This feeling centered on small but increasingly

lamentable omissions. For example, books. There was no end to
the books that I was forever promising myself to read; but,
when it came to reading them, I seemed never to have the time
or the patience. With music, too, it was the same way; the love
for it—and I suppose the indefinable need—was also there, but
not the will or opportunity to interrupt for it more than
momentarily the routine which most of us come to cherish as
existence. . . .

Now, I wanted something more than just privacy in the geographical sense. I wanted to sink roots into some replenishing
philosophy. And so it occurred to me, as the situation surrounding Advance Base evolved, that here was the opportunity. Out
there on the South Polar barrier, in cold and darkness as complete as that of the Pleistocene, I should have time to catch up,
to study and think and listen to the phonograph; and, for maybe
seven months, remote from all but the simplest distractions, I
should be able to live exactly as I chose, obedient to no necessi-
ties but those imposed by wind and night and cold, and to no
man's laws but my own. . . .

APRIL 1: GOD OF 2.5

During the four and a half months I occupied Advance Base
alone, I kept a fairly complete diary. Nearly every night, before
turning in, I sat down and wrote a thoroughgoing account of the
day's doings. Yet, I have been surprised and puzzled, on reading
the entries four years later, to find that not more of the emo-
tions and circumstances which I have always associated with the
first few days alone were actually committed to paper. For,
afterwards, it seemed that I was never busier. Although I was
up mornings before 8 o'clock and rarely went to bed before
midnight, the days weren't half long enough for me to accom-

plish the thing I set out to do. A fagged mind in the midst of a task has little patience with autobiographical trifles. As witness:

March 29

... Last night, when I finished writing, I noticed a dark patch spreading over the floor from under the stove. A bad leak had opened up in the fuel line. Worried about the fire risk, I shut off the stove and searched all through my gear for a spare line. I couldn't find one, which annoyed me; but I finally succeeded in stopping the leak with adhesive tape borrowed from the medical chest. Result: I was up until 4 o'clock this morning, most of the time damned cold, what with the fire out and the temperature at 58° below zero. The cold metal stripped the flesh from three fingers of one hand.

(Later) This being the twenty-second anniversary of the death of Captain Robert Falcon Scott, I have been reading again his immortal diary. He died on this same Barrier, at approximately the same latitude as that of Advance Base. I admire him as I admire few other men; better than most, perhaps, I can appreciate what he went through. . . .

March 30

There will be no peace until I know that the tractor party has reached Little America safely. I blame myself for having kept them here so long. Well, the radio schedule two days hence will tell the story. I've been principally occupied with putting the tunnels to rights, and not succeeding very well on account of my shoulder, which maddens me not so much from pain as from its uselessness. A fearful amount of lifting remains to be done. So far, I've managed with one hand by using my hip as a fulcrum. . . .

May was a round boulder sinking before a tide. Time sloughed off the last implication of urgency, and the days moved imperceptibly one into the other. The few world news items which Dyer read to me from time to time seemed almost as meaningless and blurred as they might to a Martian. My world was insulated against the shocks running through distant economies. Advance Base was geared to different laws. On getting up in the morning, it was enough for me to say to myself: Today is the day to change the barograph sheet, or, Today is the day to fill the stove tank. The night was settling down in earnest. By May 17th, one month after the sun had sunk below the horizon, the noon twilight was dwindling to a mere chink in the darkness, lit by a cold reddish glow. Days when the wind brooded in the north or east, the Barrier became a vast stagnant shadow surmounted by swollen masses of clouds, one layer of darkness piled on top of the other. This was the polar night, the morbid countenance of the Ice Age. Nothing moved; nothing was visible. This was the soul of inertness. One could almost hear a distant creaking as if a great weight were settling.

Out of the deepening darkness came the cold. On May 19th, when I took the usual walk, the temperature was 65° below zero. For the first time the canvas boots failed to protect my feet. One heel was nipped, and I was forced to return to the hut and change to reindeer mukluks. That day I felt miserable; my body was racked by shooting pains—exactly as if I had been gassed. Very likely I was; in inspecting the ventilator pipes next morning I discovered that the intake pipe was completely clogged with rime and that the outlet pipe was two-thirds full. Next day—Sunday the 20th—was the coldest yet. The minimum thermometer dropped to 72° below zero; the inside thermograph, which always read a bit lower than the instruments in the shelter, stood at −74°; and the thermograph in the shelter was stopped dead—the ink, though well laced with glycerine, and the lubricant were both frozen. So violently did the air in the fuel tank expand after the stove was lit that oil went shooting all over the place; to insulate the tank against similar temperature spreads I wrapped around it the rubber air cushion which by some lucky error had been included among my gear. In the glow of a flashlight the vapor rising from the stovepipe and the outlet ventilator looked like the discharge from two steam engines. My fingers agonized over the thermograph, and I was hours putting it to rights. The fuel wouldn't flow from the drums; I had to take one inside and heat it near the stove. All day long I kept two primus stoves burning in the tunnel.

Sunday the 20th also brought a radio schedule; I had the devil's own time trying to meet it. The engine balked for an hour; my fingers were so brittle and frostbitten from tinkering with the carburetor that, when I actually made contact with Little America, I could scarcely work the key. "Ask Haines to come on," was my first request. While Hutcheson searched the tunnels of Little America for the Senior Meteorologist, I chatted briefly with Charlie Murphy. Little America claimed only −60°. "But we're moving the brass monkeys below," Charlie advised. "Seventy-one below here now," I said. "You can have it," was the closing comment from the north.

Then Bill Haines's merry voice sounded in the earphones. I explained the difficulty with the thermograph. "Same trouble we've had," Bill said. "It's probably due to frozen oil. I'd suggest you bring the instrument inside, and try soaking it in gasoline, to cut whatever oil traces remain. Then rinse it in ether. As for the ink's freezing, you might try adding more glycerine." Bill was in a jovial mood. "Look at me, Admiral," he boomed. "I never have any trouble with the instruments. The trick is in having an ambitious and docile assistant." I really chuckled over that because I knew, from the first expedition, what Grimminger, the Junior Meteorologist, was going through: Bill, with his back to the fire and blandishment on his tongue, persuading the recruit that duty and the opportunity for self-improvement required him to go up into the blizzard to fix a balky trace; Bill humming to himself in the warmth of the shack while the assistant in an open pit kept a theodolite trained on the sounding balloon soaring into the night, and stuttered into a telephone the different vernier readings from which Bill was calculating the velocities and directions of the upper air currents. That day

I rather wished that I, too, had an assistant. He would have taken his turn on the anemometer pole, no mistake. The frost in the iron cleats went through the fur soles of the mukluks, and froze the balls of my feet. My breath made little explosive sounds on the wind; my lungs, already sore, seemed to shrivel when I breathed.

Seldom had the aurora flamed more brilliantly. For hours the night danced to its frenetic excitement. And at times the sound of Barrier quakes was like that of heavy guns. My tongue was swollen and sore from drinking scalding hot tea, and the tip of my nose ached from frostbite. A big wind, I guessed, would come out of this still cold; it behooved me to look to my roof. I carried gallons of water topside, and poured it around the edges of the shack. It froze almost as soon as it hit. The ice was an armor plating over the packed drift.

At midnight, when I clambered topside for an auroral "ob," a wild sense of suffocation came over me the instant I pushed my shoulders through the trapdoor. My lungs gasped but no air reached them. Bewildered and perhaps a little frightened, I slid down the ladder and lunged into the shack. In the warm air the feeling passed as quickly as it had come. Curious but cautious, I again made my way up the ladder. And again the same thing happened; I lost my breath, but I perceived why. A light air was moving down from eastward; and its bitter touch, when I faced into it, was constricting the breathing passages. So I turned my face away from it, breathing into my glove; and in that attitude finished the "ob." Before going below, I made an interesting experiment. I put a thermometer on the snow, let it lie there awhile, and discovered that the temperature at the surface was actually 5° colder than at the level of the instrument shelter, four feet higher. Reading in the sleeping bag afterwards, I froze one finger, although I shifted the book steadily from one hand to the other, slipping the unoccupied hand into the warmth of the bag.

Out of the cold and out of the east came the wind. It came

on gradually, as if the sheer weight of the cold were almost too much to be moved. On the night of the 21st the barometer started down. The night was black as a thunderhead when I made my first trip topside; and a tension in the wind, a bulking of shadows in the night indicated that a new storm center was forming. Next morning, glad of an excuse to stay underground, I worked a long time on the Escape Tunnel by the light of a red candle standing in a snow recess. That day I pushed the emergency exit to a distance of twenty-two feet, the farthest it was ever to go. My stint done, I sat down on a box, thinking how beautiful was the red of the candle, how white the rough-hewn snow. Soon I became aware of an increasing clatter of the anemometer cups. Realizing that the wind was picking up, I went topside to make sure that everything was secured. It is a queer experience to watch a blizzard rise. First there is the wind, rising out of nowhere. Then the Barrier unwrenches itself from quietude; and the surface, which just before had seemed as hard and polished as metal, begins to run like a making sea. Sometimes, if the wind strikes hard, the drift comes across the Barrier like a hurrying white cloud, tossed hundreds of feet in the air. Other times the growth is gradual. You become conscious of a general slithering movement on all sides. The air fills with tiny scraping and sliding and rustling sounds as the first loose crystals stir. In a little while they are moving as solidly as an incoming tide, which creams over the ankles, then surges to the waist, and finally is at the throat. I have walked in drift so thick as not to be able to see a foot ahead of me; yet, when I glanced up, I could see the stars shining through the thin layer just overhead.

Smoking tendrils were creeping up the anemometer pole when I finished my inspection. I hurriedly made the trapdoor fast, as a sailor might batten down a hatch; and knowing that my ship was well secured, I retired to the cabin to ride out the storm. It could not reach me, hidden deep in the Barrier crust; nevertheless the sounds came down. The gale sobbed in the ventilators, shook the stovepipe until I thought it would be jerked out by the roots, pounded the roof with sledge-hammer blows. I could actually feel the suction effect through the previous snow. A breeze flickered in the room and the tunnels. The candles wavered and went out. My only light was the feeble storm lantern.

Even so, I didn't have any idea how really bad it was until I went aloft for an observation. As I pushed back the trapdoor, the drift met me like a moving wall. It was only a few steps from the ladder to the instrument shelter, but it seemed more like a mile. The air came at me in snowy rushes; I breasted it as I might a heavy surf. No night had ever seemed so dark. The beam from the flashlight was choked in its throat; I could not see my hand before my face.

My windproofs were caked with drift by the time I got below. I had a vague feeling that something had changed while I was gone, but what, I couldn't tell. Presently I noticed that the shack was appreciably colder. Raising the stove lid, I was surprised to find that the fire was out, though the tank was half full. I decided that I must have turned off the valve unconsciously before going aloft; but, when I put a match to the burner, the draught down the pipe blew out the flame. The wind, then, must have killed the fire. I got it going again, and watched it carefully.

The blizzard vaulted to gale force. Above the roar the deep, taut thrumming note of the radio antenna and the anemometer guy wires reminded me of wind in a ship's rigging. The wind direction trace turned scratchy on the sheet; no doubt drift had short-circuited the electric contacts, I decided. Realizing that it was hopeless to attempt to try to keep them clear, I let the instrument be. There were other ways of getting the wind direction. I tied a handkerchief to a bamboo pole and ran it through the outlet ventilator; with a flashlight I could tell which way the cloth was whipped. I did this at hourly intervals, noting any change of direction on the sheet. But by 2 o'clock in the morning I had had enough of this periscope sighting. If I expected to sleep and at the same time maintain the continuity of the records, I had no choice but to clean the contact points.

The wind was blowing hard then. The Barrier shook from the concussions overhead; and the noise was as if the entire physical world were tearing itself to pieces. I could scarcely heave the trapdoor open. The instant it came clear I was plunged into a blinding smother. I came out crawling, clinging to the handle of the door until I made sure of my bearings. Then I let the door fall shut, not wanting the tunnel filled with drift. To see was impossible. Millions of tiny pellets exploded in my eyes, stinging like BB shot. It was even hard to breathe, because snow instantly clogged the mouth and nostrils. I made my way toward the anemometer pole on hands and knees, scared that I might be bowled off my feet if I stood erect; one false step and I should be lost forever.

I found the pole all right; but not until my head collided with a cleat. I managed to climb it, too, though ten million ghosts were tearing at me, ramming their thumbs into my eyes. But the errand was useless. Drift as thick as this would mess up the contact points as quickly as they were cleared; besides, the wind cups were spinning so fast that I stood a good chance of losing a couple of fingers in the process. Coming down the pole, I had a sense of being whirled violently through the air, with no control over my movements. The trapdoor was completely buried when I found it again, after scraping around for some time with my mittens. I pulled at the handle, first with one hand, then with both. It did not give. It's a tight fit, anyway, I mumbled to myself. The drift has probably wedged the corners. Standing astride the hatch, I braced myself and heaved with all my strength. I might just as well have tried hoisting the Barrier.

Panic took me then, I must confess. Reason fled. I clawed at the three-foot square of timber like a madman. I beat on it with my fists, trying to shake the snow loose; and, when that did no good, I lay flat on my belly and pulled until my hands went weak from cold and weariness. Then I crooked my elbow, put my face down, and said over and over again, You damn fool, you damn fool. Here for weeks I had been defending myself against the danger of being penned inside the shack; instead, I was now locked out; and nothing could be worse, especially since I had only a wool parka and pants under my windproofs. Just two feet below was sanctuary—warmth, food, tools, all the means of survival. All these things were at an arm's length away, but I was powerless to reach them.

There is something extravagantly insensate about an Antarctic blizzard at night. Its vindictiveness cannot be measured on an anemometer sheet. It is more than just wind: it is a solid wall of snow moving at gale force, pounding like surf.* The whole malevolent rush is concentrated upon you as upon a personal enemy. In the senseless explosion of sound you are reduced to a crawling thing on the margin of a disintegrating world; you can't see, you can't hear, you can hardly move. The lungs gasp after the air sucked out of them, and the brain is shaken. Nothing in the world will so quickly isolate a man.

Half-frozen, I stabbed toward one of the ventilators, a few feet away. My mittens touched something round and cold. Cupping it in my hands, I pulled myself up. This was the outlet ventilator. Just why, I don't know—but instinct made me kneel and press my face against the opening. Nothing in the room was visible, but a dim patch of light illuminated the floor, and warmth rose up to my face. That steadied me.

Still kneeling, I turned my back to the blizzard and considered what might be done. I thought of breaking in the windows in the roof, but they lay two feet down in hard crust, and were reinforced with wire besides. If I only had something to dig with, I could break the crust and stamp the windows in with my feet. The pipe cupped between my hands supplied the first inspiration; maybe I could use that to dig with. It, too, was

*Because of this blinding, suffocating drift, in the Antarctic, winds of only moderate velocity have the punishing force of full-fledged hurricanes elsewhere.

wedged tight; I pulled until my arms ached, without budging it; I had lost all track of time, and the despairing thought came to me that I was lost in a task without an end. Then I remembered the shovel. A week before, after leveling drift from the last light blow, I had stabbed a shovel handle up in the crust somewhere to leeward. That shovel would save me. But how to find it in the avalanche of the blizzard?

I lay down and stretched out full length. Still holding the pipe, I thrashed around with my feet, but pummeled only empty air. Then I worked back to the hatch. The hard edges at the opening provided another grip, and again I stretched out and kicked. Again no luck. I dared not let go until I had something else familiar to cling to. My foot came up against the other ventilator pipe. I edged back to that, and from the new anchorage repeated the maneuver. This time my ankle struck something hard. When I felt it and recognized the handle, I wanted to caress it.

Embracing this thrice-blessed tool, I inched back to the trapdoor. The handle of the shovel was just small enough to pass under the little wooden bridge which served as a grip. I got both hands on the shovel and tried to wrench the door up; my strength was not enough, however. So I lay down flat on my belly and worked my shoulders under the shovel. Then I heaved, the door sprang open, and I rolled down the shaft. When I tumbled into the light and warmth of the room, I kept thinking, How wonderful, how perfectly wonderful.

4

THE HORSEMAN

HALF-WAY ROUND THE WORLD ON HORSEBACK

AIMÉ FELIX TSCHIFFELY

Swiss-born, British-educated A.F. Tschiffely spent much of his life on horseback in the Argentine. A schoolteacher and adventurer, in 1926 he took to the saddle and spent two and a half years riding his way to New York. He went via Bolivia, Peru, Ecuador, Colombia, Panama, Costa Rica, San Salvador, Guatemala and Mexico. He traveled through every kind of terrain and landscape. In the Andes he rode through the clouds at 18,000 feet. The following story was related on the British Broadcasting Corporation.

It wasn't just madness or a desire for publicity that induced me to ride two horses from the extreme south of South America to the United States when comfortable ships would have taken me from point to point in three weeks or less.

The two horses I took with me were descendants of the stock which was shipped to South America by the Spanish Conquistadores about four hundred years ago. Many of them were turned loose by the Spaniards, and others managed to escape during hostile attacks by the Indians. But—owing to various circumstances—this wild breed of horses was becoming nearly extinct, and the object of my ride was to prove to the Government that it was hardy and useful and worth saving from extinction.

My journey took me two and a half years and was probably the longest expedition ever made on horseback.

I traveled over vast plains, through deserts, jungles, swamps and over lofty mountains. In one place in the Andes we were close on 18,000 feet above sea level, and then again we found ourselves in steaming tropical swamps and jungles where it was often necessary to use a bush knife to open a trail through the dense vegetation. I say "we" although I was traveling without human companionship, for—after all—my two faithful horses did most of the hard work, and if it hadn't been for their instincts and thinking, I should have come to grief on more than one occasion.

I had to go down to the far south of the Argentine Republic to find them, for I wanted a couple of animals which would be able to stand so long and arduous an expedition. There I bought thirty horses from a Tehuelche Indian Chief named "Liempichun," which means "I have feathers," and when they had been driven I chose two which looked good and tough to me.

Although they were sixteen and eighteen years old respectively, neither of these horses had ever been ridden, and you can imagine what kind of a war dance they led me when I first jumped onto their backs. Rodeo horses may be showy goat jumpers but for real unadulterated buck jumping I recommend the hurricane deck of a wild horse. However, after a great deal of patience and kindness on my part, and one or two nasty falls, the horses became more friendly and I was ready to start.

I had spent something like two years studying the road I proposed to follow and had gathered as much information about the different countries as I could. This, incidentally, was very little and vague, as I found out later.

Although I tried to avoid publicity the press soon heard about my proposed journey and the comments were many and varied. Most of the papers thought the trip was impossible and one or two said frankly that I ought to consult a doctor. Others were of the opinion that the expedition involved cruelty to animals.

If these worthy gentlemen of the press had only thought a little they might have realized that if a man sets out into the wilds with two horses, his life will depend on them to a great extent and he will make it his first duty to attend to their welfare.

Usually I rode on one horse while the other carried the pack, and I changed from one to the other whenever I thought the change would do them good. When the trail was steep or the going difficult I divided the pack between them and went on foot, for the horses made faster progress in this way and there was less danger of a nasty fall. Although I had to sleep out in the open very often, I could not carry a tent, for even the lightest would have meant extra weight for the pack horse. I often had to sleep in huts, but I much preferred to curl up somewhere in the open where there were fewer insects than are to be found in most of the habitations of Indians.

I rarely bothered about wild beasts, for most of them are afraid of man and are only too glad to keep out of his way. Crushed garlic, rubbed on a rope made of horsehair, will usually keep snakes away from a sleeping man if he places this rope in a circle around him before he lies down to sleep on the ground. The only beast of prey which might attack a man in South or Central America is the jaguar, but since it isn't found in many places, one is fairly safe.

I have read in books and heard travelers tell how they made fires all night to keep pumas away. The puma is the American lion; in North America they often call him "cougar." This animal is very cowardly but rather curious and, after all, if the nervous traveler wishes to make fires all night one can hardly blame the poor puma for that. No; the real dangers I had to face were lack of water and food; and dangerous trails in the mountains. Then there were burning deserts and steaming tropical swamps and the possibility of fever and sickness.

I once had to stay for four days in a filthy settlement where over 150 natives were down with bubonic plague, and during my stay in the place twenty-four died of this horrible disease.

The swimming of torrential mountain rivers also presents many hazards, and in some of the tropical waters one has to look out for alligators and crocodiles. Even worse than these are the small cannibal fish, called caribes or piranhas. They attack in thousands and will tear to pieces in a few seconds any human being or animal which happens to have a cut or scratch, for they are attracted by the smell of blood.

Another unpleasant customer which lurks in some of the muddy waters is an ugly flat fish; the poisonous stinging ray. The tremblador or electric eel—one of nature's most extraordinary freaks—is another very dangerous denizen of some tropical streams and rivers. The discharge of one of these living electric batteries is powerful enough to paralyze a horse and cause him to sink like lead. They are from three to five feet long and about as thick as a man's arm. As well as poisonous fish, all sorts of different poisonous herbs and weeds grow in some parts of South America, and they will kill a horse if he eats them. I came across several varieties of these herbs and had to take great care that my animals did not get them.

From Buenos Aires we set out in a northwesterly direction toward the distant Bolivian border. There are few roads in that mountainous country, so I had carefully planned to arrive in Bolivia during the dry season; for I knew that the only means of communication would be the dry river beds. I had plenty of time, so I took things easy. But I had no end of trouble with the horses for the first few days, for they were none too tame and shied at such things as houses and traffic, which they had never seen in their desolate native regions in the far south. As soon as we were out in the open pampas things became more pleasant, and Mancha and Gato—as I had called the horses—gradually became more friendly. Mancha means "Spot," and Gato "Cat."

I had two .45-caliber six-shooters strapped to my hips, and the pack horse also carried a .44 rifle and a 16-bore repeating shotgun, for I knew I would have to rely a good deal on firearms for food. The type of saddle I used was a light framework of wood covered with leather. I piled sheepskins on this and was able to use it as a comfortable bed as well as for riding.

We jogged along for days over the vast flatness, which suggested eternity. There was little wildlife to be seen except prairie owls and other birds. Herds of cattle were grazing and occasionally a *gaucho*, or Argentine cattle boy, passed us.

It got warmer as we continued north, and when we entered the huge alkali flats the sun rays seemed to penetrate to the very bones. The water is so scarce and bad there and the place is so barren, excepting for a few cactus plants and other shrubs, that I had been told that I should never get my horses across. But we managed all right and, when we came out safe and sound on the other side, I was well satisfied with my animals, for they had given the first real proof of their toughness.

At length we entered the mighty Andes, and traveled for days through vast valleys, using the dry river beds as roads and guessing our direction with more luck than judgment.

As we approached the Bolivian border we occasionally met Indians who were on their way down to distant villages or towns. Once a year—during the dry season—the hardy mountaineers make their long journeys. Their woven goods and beautifully made pottery are packed on llamas, the pretty and elegant South American beasts of burden, which they drive before them. When they have sold or exchanged their goods they return home before the rains set in and the wild rivers thunder down the deep ravines and canyons, on their way to the distant Atlantic.

The further we penetrated into this vast and imposing labyrinth of mountains the rougher and less hospitable the country became. Icy blasts swept down from the high peaks, and there was nothing green to be seen. For days we stumbled over rocks and boulders in river beds, and sometimes we threaded our way along giddy precipices where the horses had to pick their way with the greatest care.

It was bitterly cold in the high passes, and mountain sickness

—caused by the low air pressure—sometimes made my nose bleed profusely and caused a feeling of giddiness. This mountain sickness—called *sorroche* or *puna* in the Andes—often affects animals as well, and unless the traveler takes care never to overexert his mount, it may collapse and even die.

The natives in some of these regions have a very rough but quite effective cure for it. If one of their animals falls they quickly cut a gash in the roof of its mouth to bleed it and then blow a little pure alcohol up its nostrils. I never hurried my horses where the trails were steep, and gave them a rest whenever they asked for it—and I assure you that once a horse gets used to a man he learns how to ask for many things.

In many parts of Bolivia it is advisable not to drink water. It looks clear enough but it is often bad and even dangerous. The natives make themselves a strong alcoholic beverage with corn. This abounds wherever Indians live, and its preparation is original, though not very appetizing. First of all, a quantity of corn is boiled for some hours, and in the meantime more corn is chewed by the Indians. When it has been masticated into a soft paste and well mixed with saliva, they spit it into a wooden bowl. The resulting paste is called *moco,* and acts rather as yeast does in the making of bread. When the boiled corn is ready, the chewed *moco* is added to it and soon the concoction begins to fizz and bubble, and after a day or so the native beer, or *chicha,* is ready. Owing to the scarcity of good water, I had to drink quite a lot of *chicha*—and what the eye has seen the heart can grieve over.

After weeks of traveling we reached La Paz, the capital of Bolivia, and shortly afterward a bloody uprising broke out in the Indian territory which we had just left, and many whites lost their lives. In most cases my sympathy goes to the poor and oppressed Indians, who have suffered untold injustices and misery ever since the Spaniards, under Pizarro, invaded their land.

We continued north from La Paz, skirted Lake Titicaca, and finally reached Curco, the ancient capital of the Inca Empire.

Sir Francis Chichester's yacht "Gipsy Moth" ten miles out of Sydney Heads, Australia.

World Wide Photos

World Wide Photos

New Yorker, William Willis, age 71, aboard his raft after arrival at Tully, Queensland, Australia.

Colin Irwin in his 19-foot boat arriving at Kotzebue, Alaska.

The historic flight at Kitty Hawk, North Carolina, on December 17, 1903 . . . first powered plane flown by man.

The "Spirit of St. Louis" off Roosevelt field on Charles Lindbergh's historic flight to Paris.

Amelia Earhart being welcomed in New York on June 20, 1932 by Mayor James J. Walker.

Admiral Byrd (center) being welcomed in New Zealand en route to the Antartic.

Harry Roskolenko at Meckering,
Western Australia, October, 1956.

Sylvan Hart, the last of the mountain men, outside his wilderness
home beside the Salmon River,
Idaho.

Tom Neale on his own idyllic island in 1972.

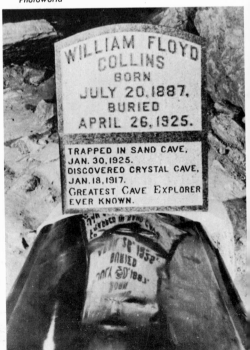

Casket of Floyd Collins, the greatest cave explorer known.

Maurice Herzog of *Annapurna* fame at Idlewild Airport in New York.

Tazieff before the "Craters of Fire".

Eric Shipton when *not* climbing Mt. Everest.

J. R. L. Anderson, author of "The Ulysses Factor".

This lake is some 14,000 feet above sea level and, although it does not look very big on the map, it took me a week to ride along its full length, from south to north. In this neighborhood we passed several most interesting ruins, which date back to Incaic and pre-Incaic times, and, although I am a keen student of archaeology, I could not stay in these regions as long as I would like to have done. From there we swung due west and entered another terrific network of mountains—frightfully rough country where nature works on so gigantic a scale that if often made me gasp.

When we were on the mountaintops it was bitterly cold, and when we had stumbled down over neck-breaking trails into steaming tropical valleys, swarms of mosquitoes attacked us, whilst flocks of parrots screeched as if protesting against our invasion. Sometimes we had to cross Indian hanging bridges across deep chasms. When we came to the first of these hammocklike structures, which sagged dangerously in the middle, I thought my horses would never get across it, but the animals picked their way with great care, and when the bridge swayed too much they stopped until it was safe to proceed. Some of these bridges were only about three feet wide, and I always unsaddled the horses and took them across singly, for I did not think these wobbly and giddy pieces of primitive engineering would have stood the weight of two horses. I sometimes feared that one animal would be too much for these frail but daring constructions.

Once, while we were following a narrow trail, one of the horses lost his foothold and shot down a steep incline to what looked like certain death. Luckily, however, his descent was stopped by a solitary tree on the very edge of a deep precipice. It was not at all an easy job to rescue him, but he seemed to realize the danger for he never moved until ropes and lassos had been tied to him and he had been pulled back to safety with the assistance of friendly Indians.

Eventually we reached Lima, the capital of Peru, and from there we continued north along the coast.

We had to travel through sandy deserts where the heat was terrific. It never rains in these coastal regions and water can only be found where rivers come down from the Andes. One desert which we had to cross was ninety-six miles from river to river; a dangerous journey which took us twenty hours to accomplish. We did most of the traveling at night but, since we could only do this when there was a moon to help us, we often had to forge ahead during the daytime, when the tropical sun baked the sand to such a degree that I could feel it burn through my heavy riding boots.

Often I rode for miles over the wet sands along the beach where thousands of sea birds circled above us. The monotony of the scenery and the regular breaking of the waves often made me feel very sleepy and I found it very difficult to keep awake. When we came nearer to the equator I again changed the route and took to the mountains once more. It was cooler there, though the broken country made progress very slow. But I had had enough of deserts, heat and quicksands along the Peruvian coast, and had no desire to attempt crossing the low swampland along the coast of Ecuador.

Up and down wound our trail, sometimes through dense vegetation in hot, tropical valleys, where the horses had to wade through deep mud, and where we had to be on the lookout for mud holes. These and quicksands are very dangerous traps; they are extremely difficult to distinguish from the rest of the ground, and should the traveler happen to blunder onto one of them he will be sucked down and perish unless help is at hand.

Once the horse I was riding refused to go a step further, and the more I tried to urge him on the fussier he became. When I finally used my spurs he reared up and snorted, but still refused to go forward. Luckily an Indian who spoke Spanish appeared on the scene and told me that I was on the very edge of a dangerous mud hole. How my horse sensed the danger is really mysterious, for there were none of these mud holes in his native regions. He probably saved my life, anyway, for I remember how a mounted guide, who once worked for me, trod on one of these places. His pony at once sank in, and if I had not carried lassos and ropes it would never have got free. As it was, we had a very difficult and exciting time pulling the poor beast out.

I was very proud and pleased when we crossed the equator not far from Quito, the capital of Ecuador. Strange as it may seem, it was very cool there, for we were high above sea level, and near us towered several beautiful snow-capped peaks and volcanoes, their snows glittering in the dark blue sky.

The Indians in every region through which we passed varied a lot in dress and general appearance, and many were the languages they spoke. If they did not understand any Spanish I had to make myself understood by signs, and this was often none too easy and required a great deal of patience.

Colombia was not an easy nut to crack but we finally reached the shores of the Caribbean Sea at the extreme north of South America. We had been on the road just about one year. The rainy season had now set in, and in many places we had to do almost as much swimming as walking—at least so it seemed to me at the time. Once, during a severe thunderstorm, I was knocked off my mount and stunned by a flash of lightning, but luckily I was not much hurt.

The overland trip from the north of Colombia to Panama is impossible because of swamps and impenetrable jungles and so I was obliged to embark the horses as far as Cristobal, near the Panama Canal. We stayed hereabouts for nearly a month and a half—about the longest stay I made anywhere—until the rains subsided and the jungles had dried up. Then I saddled up and set out again toward the forests and dense jungles which lie between Panama and Costa Rica. For several weeks we fought our way through dense vegetation and dark forests. We had to cross an 11,000-foot mountain range from which I could see both the Pacific and Atlantic oceans, and the jungles below us looked like another angry sea of green.

In some parts it was very difficult to find food and I often fed off parrots, wild turkeys, wood pigeons and similar birds, and occasionally a wild pig provided me with meat. But I was once so hard up for food that I had to shoot and eat monkeys, though it made me feel like a common murderer, and the meat was extremely tough. My menu was often a strange one, and among other rare dishes I have had to eat large lizards, or iguanas as they are called in Latin America; crocodile, horse meat, ostrich eggs, armadillo; and even a snake once figured on my bill of fare. The latter tasted rather like a mixture of chicken and fish, and in some parts it is considered a delicacy by the native gourmets.

The horses had their share of strange fodder, too, for grass does not grow everyhere. They also provided unwilling food for others, for in the jungle, ticks, vampire bats and many other pests made life unpleasant for them. Some of the South American vampire bats are much bigger than the useful European bats and, though they never bothered me, I had no end of trouble when they attacked my horses. The big ones can suck as much as half a pint of blood, and if a few of these repulsive creatures get at a horse they weaken him terribly. But I soon found a way of protecting my two pets against vampires and ticks, and managed to keep them healthy and strong.

What with jungles and revolutions, I had plenty of excitement in Central America, and later, when I thought the rest of the journey would be just plain sailing, I ran into more revolutions in Mexico, where I had a very lively time of it. Fighting and banditry obliged me to make a big detour over the mountains and, in spite of the delay caused by this, we slowly approached our goal. I soon found out that a pleasant smile will take a man further than all the guns will, and somehow I managed to wriggle through without worse consequences than a black eye and a bullet through my saddle sheepskin.

When things became too hot the Mexican Government provided me with military escorts who accompanied me through the most dangerous parts. Long before I had reached that country the authorities and people knew about my ride, and since Mexicans are keen horsemen and lovers of the open, our long journey appealed to them, and they saw to it that nothing should happen to us on our way through their beautiful but turbulent country. After we had crossed the Rio Grande into Texas things were easy, but the further we went the heavier the traffic became. Finally I unsaddled in New York, and we took a ship back to the Argentine.

Thanks to delays caused by an official reception, I missed sailing on the ill-fated *Vestris*, which sank with over a hundred lives lost. We left the United States in the next boat, and you may be sure that I did not leave my two horses behind but took them back home with me on a comfortable passenger liner.

Thus they lived again to see their beloved pampas, where they were turned loose to roam from horizon to horizon and enjoy the life that is natural to them. They had done their duty!

5

THE POET

ALL AROUND THE WORLD ON A SCOOTER

HARRY ROSKOLENKO

It was the spring of 1956 and I was in Paris, briefly enjoying the lush Parisian weather after a cold, wet winter. But despite my nostalgia for the idyllic season, I was leaving Paris for places known and unknown. I said a sentimental good-bye and took to the high road on a motorized safari.

My somewhat cynical friends, when toasting my adventure-in-progress, had insisted that it was physically impossible to complete, unless I was a space cadet; that the daily dangers and difficulties I would encounter would stop me in my tracks before I had gone 1000 miles. I was, in fact, going around the world on a Vespa motorscooter. I would visit Genoa, Athens, Istanbul, Teheran, Karachi, Bombay and Colombo, where I would embark for Perth and then scooter across the grim Nullarbor desert toward Melbourne and the Olympic Games. After that, I would go to San Francisco and scooter home to New York.

Of course, I was completely unprepared for this adventure on two small wheels. In my twenties, however, I had been an athlete and I recalled, heroically, as if to bolster my courage, the many times that I had run against world-famous runners like Paavo Nurmi and Willy Ritola.

But, as I grew older, I gave up track, preferring to get my

exercise through my typewriter, as a journalist and novelist, occasionally reaching for a handy bottle of Scotch, which hardly required too many vigorous movements. I became the sitting-down man instead of the doing man, content to grow flabby as I watched younger men adventure with the times.

But one Parisian morning I had made a decision. I packed two duffle bags and became a scootering gypsy, adrift on the high-roads of the world.

I carried 100 pounds of camping equipment, clothes for all sorts of weather, my ancient typewriter and a Graflex camera, ready for everything as I wandered the routes once taken by Ghengis Khan and Charlemagne.

I was to be king of the scooter, an emperor of ruts, the prince of the open country and the servant of my own eyes and spirit.

Leaving democratic, pastoral France and Italy, I saw the totalitarian gardens of Yugoslavia. In rugged, mountainous Greece, where mythical Olympian gods once played their Grecian games, the roads led through ancient civilizations.

Having accepted a challenge, I was soon in the middle of an exotic world, eagerly experiencing the excitements that made each day magical with wonder and drama.

I learned about roads from the ground up. I knew the good and the bad, the indifferent and the impossible as I scootered over sand, gravel, mud and the terrifying mountains of Greece, Turkey, Iran, Pakistan and India.

I went through roadless worlds, with monsoons for my umbrella and 200-pound dogs making murderous passes at me.

I was an unscheduled traveler, uncertain of many things, yet coping with adventure and misadventure alike.

One night, in the high mountains of Turkish Kurdistan, I used my Vespa engine to fight off a pack of wolves. I revved up the motor, exploding it like a tommy gun, and the wolves took to the hills.

At Thermopylae I encountered jovial, water-pipe-smoking peasants sitting under olive trees, with nothing evident of the historical, warring past of Thermopylae. Yet death appeared everywhere, for dogs, cats, donkeys and snakes were constantly being run down by the huge transports speeding through the pass as if it were a racetrack.

I thought of the Greek tragic sense of life, for a man riding a fragile vehicle is subject to man's and nature's whims. Such accidental encounters and mishaps on wet, windy mountains gave me a new respect for the more prudent adventurer, which I was not.

But when I saw another carefree man riding his monkey on his donkey, near snowclad Fourka Pass, and I heard gypsies singing, I forgot Greek tragedy, tragic Agamemnon and thundering Zeus, and I dreamed of diaphanous Daphne instead.

Red-billed soaring cranes swooped over me as I approached the Narthakian Hills, where I rode for hours through rain, thunder and lightning.

On two occasions I stampeded flocks of sheep en route to their enclosures, as well as a donkey with a sheep perched on the saddle. The piquant hitchhiker looked at me strangely, likely convinced that I looked even more bizarre on my earless scooter.

I saw antique Olympia, the ancient source of the modern Olympic Games. Marbled antiquity enveloped me as I tripped over classical debris, going past the Roman bath, where no one bathed, past the altar of Zeus, where no one prayed, pausing long at the excavation of the Stadia, where the last Olympian athletes had competed 1700 years ago. Later the rivers Kladeus and Alpheius overran their banks, burying Olympia's relics of pomp under 20 feet of mud.

In Turkey, minarets and smokestacks joined images, looking strange under the cypress trees that lined the rugged road. Old huts, made of crisscrossed wooden slats, sagged alongside of newly built pink stone houses. Brightly pantalooned women and girls, with white burnooses, were working in the adjacent fields of rye.

A sudden sound arrested everything, as two huge bullocks locked horns. A large tortoise moped by, prodded on by two laughing boys carrying laden copper tea trays to the workers in the fields.

Peasant wagons, looking like big wicker baskets, were endlessly on the move.

In one town my scooter almost caused a miniature riot, with the delightful children happy to turn their assorted talents to scooter engineering as they helped me change my fouled spark plug.

One night my scooter and I spent the night at the edge of a Turk encampment, with sheep, donkeys, dogs and goats inspecting my machine, when not nibbling at my groundsheet as I slept. By morning the sheet had been nicely chewed at.

In modern Ankara I had the sheet repaired at a jewelry shop that also operated as a rendezvous for shoppers for secondhand camping equipment, with sagelike amateur sportsmen offering me advice on how to fight off a wolf that had not had its daily ration of succulent sheep.

Near Mount Ararat, I spent a few days with Kurdish peasants, fishing in their high mountain streams with an Arab net. A violent hailstorm came up as I left, followed by enormous arcs of double rainbows that illuminated the entire sky. It was a spectacle of biblical naturalness, exaggerating the height of Ararat's 17,000 feet. Twin-peaked Ararat divided Turkey from Iran and the Soviet Union and was a gaunt playground for Turkish soldiers, who occasionally maneuvered around it, and for mountain climbers anxious to add another mountain to their list of accomplishments. It was as formidable as it was barren, but beyond it lay the green Garden of Eden.

Before Mount Ararat, I had gone through Zigana Pass. A pass can divide civilizations, and this was mountain, lumbering land, with men in overcoats and heavy turbans stacking pine logs under snow-covered sheds. Yellow azaleas banked the slopes, also alight with patches of orchid rhododendron. Waterfalls tumbled out of the mist from the adjacent hills, glittering through the trees, appearing in the fog like tall feathers. At Urman Harvesi, halfway up the summit of Zigana Pass, the clouds darkened, ready for rain and snow, ready to sink the mud-and-earthen road and shut off transportation and communication to the civilization down at the next town.

It was getting dark and I was miles from a town, dragging slowly through the snowy, freezing pass, my weakened light hardly penetrating the darkness. When the battery finally gave out, I used my flashlight, holding it in my right hand along with the ever-changing accelerator; for I was shifting from first into second and back every hundred yards through the mountains. But it became much too dangerous, for my stiffened fingers ceased to respond. I knew that if I continued, I was inviting something, and I had gone almost 5000 miles without a serious accident. But I was cold and hungry, and the next town was miles below, in the darkness of the valley. I quit when I saw a cavelike hollow in the side of the mountain and pushed my scooter to the entrance to block off the cold wind.

My emergency rations had been used up frivolously, some given to children who had pushed me when I could not get started, so I went hungry. Then the damp cold got worse. There was no firewood and nothing to burn on the snowy mountain, for I was way above the timberline. I burned my special beat-off-the-dogs stick, then all of my matches, and I listened to the water dripping in the cave, imagining the walls would soon fall in and box me up for eternity.

Then I heard something, and I sweated. I pointed my flashlight at the scooter-blocked entrance, but saw nothing—nothing that I could not hear better: the howling of wolves not too far off, the ominous baying echoing through the cave.

Should I ride down to Koyans? Would the scooter really block out the pack? Then I remembered wolf tales my father used to tell me as a boy, about his 12 years in the czar's army in Siberia. I remembered also that a few days earlier a Turkish army officer had told me how one of his friends, stationed at a lonely outpost, had been chewed up alive the previous winter. Nor were wolves confined to the mountains, he assured me. They often roamed the streets of the most civilized towns of eastern Turkey. I thought of Ilya, the Greek, bearing me a gift of a gun, which I had stupidly refused.

I started the motor of the scooter. It roared, exploding a barrage of monoxide that was soon filling up the cave. I stopped it and flashed my light; there on the rim of light the wolves sat and howled. I was a sweating mass of fears as I huddled into myself. Then, aiming the scooter's exhaust out toward the pack, again I started the motor, revving it up and exploding it like a machine gun. I had found a weapon, a powerful noisemaker, but a weapon which could kill me too with its fumes. It exploded its furies whenever I revved it up—but what if the spark plug got fouled or the fuel ran out? I had fuel enough for a hundred miles or four hours on a good road; but I wasn't riding, just revving. With the scooter's exhaust holding the wolves at bay, I stood there, thinking, praying, freezing yet soaked in sweat, and when the fumes became too strong, I cut the motor down for a few moments, peering at the pack through the darkness to judge their reaction, listening to their howling, then revving, revving, revving, revving, all through the four-lettering night.

By morning I was maddened with talking to myself. I had made speeches to God, to nature, to the wolves. I talked of many intimate things, remembering my divorce, wondering about her . . . blaming her for this insane voyage to death; and I remembered my Paris good-bye . . . and I knew all of my own sins, my transgressions and omissions, and why God had forsaken me.

It was light; the pack had gone, its snow tracks pointing down the side of the mountain. I looked at the tracks to see where they headed. It was not toward Koyans.

Now I drank some of my cognac and warmed up for a few

minutes. Had I drunk it during the night, I would have fallen
asleep in the cold, and the motor would not have been revved.
But most of my gas was gone. I coasted to Koyans, found a hotel
and slept for 12 pack-haunted hours.

In Erzerum I was the guest of the American Military Field
Team, hunting boar and bear for one long weekend of shooting,
which also included horon dancing and other Turkish delights.

In Iran I felt the extremes of sun, heat and desert; saw fact
and fiction dressed up in picturesque Persian garments. One
night, in Nishipur, I camped alongside the tomb of Omar
Khayyám, feeling the great poet's presence all about me in the
nearby groves and chennar trees.

A few days earlier a railroad spur had joined Nishipur to
Teheran, and the result was a startling contrast of donkey and
camel with the General Electric diesel engine, a halting balance
of East and West.

Omar Khayyám, with prophetic wizardry, had written the
following 800 years earlier:

> *With them the seed of wisdom did I sow,*
> *And with my own hand labour'd it to grow;*
> *And this was all the harvest that I reap'd—*
> *I came like water, and like the wind I go.*

In the town of Meshed, near the Afghan border, the opium
poppy left all the signs of the smoker in its wake. I smelled it
in the pulsating winds, its sickening sweetness congealing in the
air. Meshed itself lay only 50 air miles from the Soviet border,
which added a sense of political discomfort to the atmosphere.
But Meshed had a holy mission, being one of the holier places
in the Moslem world. The Eighth Imam, known as Imam Reza,
a prophet revered by the sect of Shia Moslems, was buried in
Meshed, and Moslems from various parts of the world made a
yearly visit to his tomb. Nearby, too, was ancient Tus, which had
been put to the sword by Ghengis Khan. I was in the world of

the Bible, where the past collided with the present and returned to the past again. . . .

India turned out to be a garden with many stone gods, its
people steeped in mysticism and poverty. The old India of great
temples, lush greenery and holy animals came into violent jux-
taposition with the new India emerging into our times.

The monsoon was in full season, making a liquid veil of India's
natural glories. I slept in Dak huts for two shillings a night,
which made it cheaper than a tent—and drier.

I had three weeks in India's gardens of the mind, going from
Bombay and Bangalore down to Ceylon, where I had my first
accident, being sideswiped by a bus. I came out of it without any
broken bones, though my scooter had its back bent in the encounter.

In a few days I was on the road again, reaching the last stages
of my land journey. My camera made a permanent record as I
camped and hunted in this world of antiquity. I ate the local
foods, from shaslik to shaslik, which seemed to be the inevitable
dish. I drank vodka and ouzo, becoming part of every country
as I freewheeled on my scooter, camping my way towards Melbourne and the Olympic Games. When I reached Colombo late
in August, I had traveled about 14,000 miles in less than four
months. I had seen and known thousands of memorable things,
and I had stored away material for a dozen books.

Three weeks later, I was in Perth, prepared to scoot across the
grim Nullarbor desert. And in the saltbush near Ceduna, I celebrated my 49th birthday with four aborigines, who toasted me
with a swig from my bottle of cognac.

I was lean, bronzed, healthy and happy, and with Melbourne's festive air embracing me with its Olympic spirit, I was
once again seeing records broken in the challenge that keeps
the spirit young and vital—the challenge to yourself.

6

THE HERMITS

THE LAST OF THE MOUNTAIN MEN

Harold Peterson

For the past 39 years a 20th-century frontiersman named Sylvan Hart has lived an 18th-century life in the wilderness of Idaho.

On the River of No Return, in the country named Light on the Mountains, there lives a gray-bearded man who has turned back time. At Five Mile Bar, beyond which no human soul dwells, Jedediah Smith and Christopher Carson have but recently passed by, and the year is 1844 forever.

As a young man, dismayed by fragmentation of the frontiers, the old one had rejected civilization and marched off into this farthest fastness armed with a few staples, one ax, one rifle and one degree from the University of Oklahoma. There, in the last wilderness, where one winter's snows might fall into another's before a visitor came, he became the last of the mountain men. Soon to be known as Buckskin Bill, he fashioned his own clothes of deerskin. He constructed adobe-covered buildings with hand-hewn timbers. He mined copper, smelted it, refined it and made utensils. He even made his own flintlock rifles, boring them on an ingenious handmade machine, to "save the bother of store-bought ammunition." To pay for infrequent trips to Burgdorf (pop. summer 6, winter 0), where he purchased only powder, books and Darjeeling tea, he panned gold.

Told in past years, this story would have had the most satis-factory and surprising of endings. That man, the teller could have said, lives still at the confluence of Big Five Mile Creek and the savage Salmon River. But more recently, as befits any leg-end whose substance has survived to the last third of the 20th century, it was threatened with an ironic sequel. Sylvan Hart— for that is really and truly his name—seemed in danger of being evicted from his chosen wilderness for the very reason that it was choice wilderness and the federal government had recognized it should be preserved. As a "Primitive Area," it would not be open to habitation—not even by a real mountain man.

Does this mean, then, that the majority of Americans, who have occasionally fantasied—often for as long as 30 or 40 min-utes after rereading Walden—*living as Hart lives, are to be denied any underlying reality whatsoever to their imaginings? That would be a wretched admission indeed for a nation whose character depends in no small part on the myth that a man may live thus if he chooses. The Forest Service ultimately agreed that one individual living as an authentic frontiersman deserved to continue as a kind of museum piece in himself.*

To see what had been saved, I traveled the great river to Five Mile Bar, hoping to find the myth of total self-sufficiency not yet entirely obsolete. The trip led into remote territory. Idaho has at least one county—bigger than six states—where the largest town is a ghost town. Boise, the state's biggest city at 34,393, is 145 miles from the Salmon but is the nearest reasonably com-plete outfitting point. McCall (pop. 1,440), jumping-off point for the wilderness areas, is some 60 miles by bad road and trail from Hart's dwelling. Getting there means a two-and-a-half-hour drive to the ghostly gold-mining town of Warren, then a rugged 14-hour hike over 20 miles of trail.

That route might have been simpler, but the river was guar-anteed high enough to render the south-side path dangerous and to prevent Hart from paddling across to ferry me from the better north-bank trail. By river it had to be, but there was still time in plenty to speculate about what might be waiting. Somehow I kept thinking of Johnny-Behind-the-Rocks, an early Idaho recluse noted for having never bathed or removed an article of clothing; his infrequent new garments were put on over the old ones. Named for standing off a whole troop of Indians at his cave door in the Nez Percé War of '77, Johnny died in a hospital bed in 1915 from the shock of receiving his first bath.

The boat jolted over the last rapid and rounded the last bend in the river chasm, whereupon a strangely tropical-looking compound swung into view. As the boat drifted around in the swift current, a long-bearded, helmeted and bespectacled figure appeared on the white sand beach. It laughed the uproarious, raucous laughter of the mountaineer, doubling over in its mirth and slapping its knees. "Ha! Aha!" snorted Sylvan Hart, and his voice sounded rusty, as if from disuse.

The boat had not been beached 20 seconds before Hart had begun firing up a huge, ornate samovar with a two-foot-high chimney, had explained that samovar meant "self boiler" in Russian (as opposed to Samoyed, "which denotes either 'dog' or 'Russian savage' and means 'self eater'—these savages supposedly ate humans, that's why they're self eaters") and had launched from that into a dissertation on the civilizing influence of the fur trade in Russia.

The samovar was so remarkably crafted it was not clear until much later that Hart had made it. I did, however, comment on the copper squirrels scurrying over its top. Hart seized upon the opportunity to observe that they were gray squirrels, which can dodge flintlock rifle fire, and that their eyes were beads made in India by some 11th-century process: "The design was later copied by a Frenchman who got an Indian dagger in the kidney for his trouble."

As soon as the juniper-wood fuel had started boiling the tea

water, Hart leapt up again. "I must show you my football uni-
form," he said, bounding into his kitchen house. Hart emerged,
dressed in bearskin shorts, bearskin jerkin, horned copper helmet, brass boar medallion on shiny brass chain and brandishing
a fearsome brass-handled sword. "I'll be captain," he said.
"We'll beat the varsity, and I'd like you to take some pictures
to send to my little relations. They've never seen me."

Amid this frontal assalt on credulity, Hart interjected a story
to the effect that a mountain lion, just before my arrival, had
killed and buried a doe outside his garden gate, returning two
consecutive nights to finish it off. "There we were, the two of
us," Hart said. "I was out there to guard my garden, the cougar
was lying just outside to guard his kill." This was no joke. Hart
pointed out a fresh, round cougar pawprint in the ground, the
remnants of the unfortunate victim, the brush the cat had
pawed over it and the depression where the lion had bedded
down. "Lots of people live a whole lifetime," Sylvan observed,
"without having a mountain lion in their garden."

Fact is hard to separate from fancy on Five Mile Bar, the facts
tend to be so fancy. The elk-antler door handles would be a
good case in point, except that there are so many others. It is
difficult to believe, looking around the compound, that practically every ingenious element of its orderly clutter was fashioned by Hart's hand, and the degree to which everything is
made and placed for some specific purpose is something more
than ingenious. Even the pastel red of the buildings, achieved
by using an iron compound in the homemade plaster, is designed to harmonize with the complementary pastel greens of
surrounding apple and apricot trees.

The effect enhances an already esthetic, if rampantly eclec-
tic, architecture. Kitchen house and blacksmith shop, linked in
a Tennessee dogtrot pattern, are in turn joined to the two-
storied, balconied living quarters, a modified Swiss structure, by
an open South Seas roof house. Those living quarters, by the
way, demand further mention. The lower room, masoned of

native stone, serves as winter quarters. The frame upper floor, Buckskin's summer house, boasts a bay window—a B-18 Plexiglas cockpit canopy he packed in on his back. It also has, in the balcony, a fine place to sleep in fair weather and good protection for firewood in foul. Over it all whips and cracks a picturesquely indomitable 48-star flag, its fabric faded by sun and frayed by wind. "Oh, I'm patriotic," says Buckskin. "Ever' time a bald eagle flies by, I take off my hat."

Of furnishings within the compound, only two are partial ringers: the rocking chair came around Cape Horn in the gold rush, and the table is made from the oak flooring of a building in the ghost town of Dixie. Otherwise, even the pole-picket fence enclosing the 200-by-100-foot plot is totally indigenous. Occasional pickets are much higher than the others, because "deer look up at those tall pickets, think the whole fence is that high and decide they can't jump it." The gates, which swing on marble ball bearings, are mounted with bells, not so much to sound pretty as to prevent bears from raiding the garden. "One time a bear knocked down a gate," explained Hart, "came in, picked out a sheep foot I was pickling in sulfuric acid and ate it."

Buckskin enjoyed imagining the bear's discomfiture. "Hee, hee, hee," he chuckled, wriggling in his chair. This is a characteristic expression of amusement, just as stroking his beard to a point is an expression of reflective thought. The beard, parenthetically, is a beauty, being red at the sides, white at the chin and straw-colored at the tip. Nothing, in fact, is uncolorful about Sylvan Ambrose Hart, this one-sixteenth-Apache who was born in Indian Territory in 1906, one year before it became Oklahoma. (Born in Stone, a town now vanished without a trace.) Not the nasal, reedy accent—smacking strongly of Arkansas, with its conversion of o's into broad a's (sparrah, arrah). Certainly not the vocabulary, ranging from pure dialect to free use of words like "syndrome" (in discussing Soviet economist Liberman).

Hart soon bounded up again to show off his stock of sporting goods. "This here is my skis," he said, having herded me to a storeroom at the customary trot. "I discovered birch was best for slipperiness and hog hide was best to keep from sliding backward on hills." Buckskin also displayed bows, arrahs, cross-bows, pack frames, wicker fishing creels, fly rods and highly crafted snowshoes, but his interest skipped to his boats: "This is my canoe, and someday I may make a kayak out of that elk hide over there." We then loped out to the beach, where I was to survey his rowboat, whose name, ΧΑΡΩΝ, is emblazoned on its prow. Charon, you may or may not recall, was the dread boat-man who ferried dead souls across the River Styx. On the River of No Return, the symbolism was not obscure.

Of almost equal antiquity is one of Hart's prize enthusiasms, an ancient cave once inhabited by red men long since vanished into a realm less celebrated than that of Charon's patrons. "See that soot on the cave roof?" he asked after we had scrambled the few hundred feet to prehistory. "It's so old you can't possi-bly rub it off." You can't.

"There are two feet of kitchen midden here," said Hart, pointing to a deep fire hole. "The first thing we want to know is how old it is. We reach down in here. . . ." Sylvan did so, pulling out a handful of beach sand and charcoal. "I sent this to be carbon-dated, and found out it goes back to 226 B.C. Think of it. The Great Wall of China was being built, Hannibal was a great man."

Hart jarred me back into 1966. "Let's take a look at the bomb shelter," he said cheerfully. "We might be attacked and you wouldn't know where to go." Sure enough, near his house he had blasted, bit by bit, an underground shelter out of solid rock. Sylvan smiled, looking up and down the empty Salmon River, as he said that he, unlike some others, would allow all his fara-way neighbors to use his shelter.

The two caves characterize Hart, a man living in several centuries simultaneously, an unassayable amalgam of romanti-cism, risibility and rank realism.

"Like some lunch?" Buckskin suddenly asked, apparently deciding that I had had as much edification as any man could stand between meals. "Better take it. Here among the savages you never know when you might get fed." He produced a waxy cheesecloth bag containing what he identified as "a putty of beef tallow." "Put it into hot water and it's ready to eat," he prescribed. "Add some rum, sugar, treacle, anything. Got to have concentrated food."

This was not to be our lunch, it developed. In lieu of rum-laced beef tallow, a prodigiously potent mince pie served as our concentrated nourishment. Principal ingredients were whiskey, plum preserves, raisins, dried apples, treacle and an egregiously gamy meat.

"Like the crust?" beamed Sylvan. "I make it with special pastry flour and bear grease. Bear grease doesn't have the objectionable qualities of any other grease."

After exhibiting the champagne bottle he uses as a rolling pin, Sylvan trotted into the kitchen house to show off his bottled bear grease and bear cracklings, as well as apple butter, eggs-and-beets and canned elk. "I generally get twenty-five quarts of grease per bear," he said.

Hart usually settles for shooting one bear every two years. Alternate years he takes one elk. "Meat from that one animal lasts me pr' near to June," he says. "Course, I smoke most of it."

In the case of a bear, Sylvan will gut and skin the carcass, laying the hide aside to be tanned. Next he cuts off the fat, renders it in a huge Dutch oven outside and seals it up in jars. Then he rubs smoke salt over the meat—perhaps 200 pounds of it—and after a couple of days hooks it into the smoke hole back of his fireplace.

Hart fishes, too. Using salmon flies, handline and bullets for sinkers, he catches whitefish, steelhead, bull trout, cutthroat and rainbows, which he has fresh or smokes, bakes and eats with goat cheese and tea. If he doesn't catch his first fish within a minute or two, he quits for the day.

"The trouble with this water is that it's too clean. No minerals.

All the old mountaineers had goiter: the beard concealed that. Same way in Switzerland. One group of Swiss live so far up in the mountains they still speak Latin. There, if you don't speak Latin or have a goiter, you're a barbarian."

To supplement his larder, Hart also has grouse, fool hens and snowshoe rabbits (besides some imported beef). Even a couple of mountain lions have got themselves eaten. "The meat tastes like turkey," Bill claims, "and of course it's light. Animals that eat other animals always have light meat. Animals that eat grass have dark meat." And occasionally wildcats or lynxes—"We get them big as deer around here"—bent on raiding the chicken coop find their way, indirectly, into Bill's diet. He shoots them, grinds them up and feeds them to his banties, which have developed a terrible bloodlust for fresh meat.

The area also abounds in rattlesnakes, which Hart shoots but does not eat. The snakes thrive on the warm air seeping up through fissures from deep in the canyon. In compensation, mosquitoes, gnats, flies and vermin of any description are rare or nonexistent. "Only had houseflies the last five years," growls Sylvan. "Someone finally brought us in a few." Even bacteria and viruses languish and die. They certainly find no lodgement in Hart's innards: Sylvan, who drinks little or not at all, gargles daily with 151-proof Hudson's Bay Company rum, the rocket fuel that won the north.

Instead of mosquitoes and flies, Buckskin is visited regularly by bighorn sheep, elk, bear and deer. "These animals are the same as most people, or better," says Sylvan undefensively. "Go down Seventh Avenue in New York and you can see people, but you can't talk to them. You'd be better off seeing animals. Except you could talk to the animals without 'bothering' them."

Hart has time to enjoy these creatures because his is a life stripped of all non-purposeful work. "I work three, four hours before it gets hot, then *maybe* two more after the sun goes down," says Sylvan. "Or I might just stop and watch an otter play. If you lived in a place like this and had to work hard eight hours a day, you'd be a pitiful incompetent."

A number of Hart's working hours go into his home-shot and home-sewn—but not homespun—wardrobe. "Textiles are no good," he said. "A woman could spin and knit all day without keeping her family in socks. But bearskin clothing wouldn't be wearing out just ever' little while. It takes a couple weeks' time to cut and sew a suit of buckskin, but you see this? This is my first buckskin jacket. Thirty years old and it's good as new.

"Now, what is there about buckskin you could get better on Park Avenue or Bond Street?" Sylvan continued, rhetorically, laying out a newer jacket for inspection, bullet holes in the leather neatly mended. "Just this: a cold wind is what kills you in the mountains, but it can't cut through a big stag hide. And buckskin protects you from thorns. Know what those fringes are for? Not for decoration. They let water run off faster, and they make you a poorer target by breaking up the outline.

"One thing about buckskin, though," Hart added. "If you've got a legal skin, you're in trouble. An illegal skin is homogeneous and thick all over. One killed during the hunting season has prominent veins—necessary to support all that hair—and veins are the first place the leather will crack."

Bill turned to the trousers. "The great mistake in making pants," he said, "is putting the seam on the inside of the leg. If it gets wet when you have to walk somewhere, it can take the skin right off." Next came mukluks and moccasins and shoemaking tools. "If you need a moccasin real quick," he advised, "get yourself a fresh elk or moose, cut off its heel and tie the toe."

What Hart actually does when he has a fresh elk or whatever is to scrape off fascia from the inside of the hide with fleshing knives and then marinate the hide in salt and sulfuric acid. "This mixture gets rid of the gelatin in the leather," he explains. When Hart wants to produce colored leather, he uses older methods of tanning. Chopped fine and boiled, sumac makes red leather, alder bark black, mahogany brown. Coffee grounds provide another color, and ashes give white.

Besides the old buckskin jacket, Hart owns an equally magnificent coat. The back is bear and beaver, the front wolf and badger, with calfskin over the shoulders to turn water. One sleeve is skunk, the other bear, and two pheasant hides adorn the whole. When Bucksin volunteered for World War II, the coat went with him.

The military couldn't have been any more surprised by Sylvan than the Idaho state income-tax office, which made the colossal mistake of sending Hart a whole series of letters saying he hadn't paid his taxes. Buckskin finally got dressed in his best stag skins and coonskin cap, took along a rifle and ample supply of provisions and presented himself at the tax office. "I surrender," he told the slack-jawed bureaucrats. They sent him home and promised fervently never to bother him again.

"Now, bedding," Bill announced. "Here's an elk hide I tanned. That's as good for sleeping as anything. It's warm, the hair is hollow so you can stand to have it against you, and it doesn't absorb moisture."

The guns with which Buckskin bags these trophies, trinkets and trousers have aroused considerable avarice. One handmade flintlock rifle, a particularly enviable product of loving craftsmanship, so excited a visiting Los Angeles businessman that he practically ordered Bill to sell it. When Bill turned down $1,000 and then a blank check, the man raged: "Damn it, you need the money. You *do* use money, don't you?"

"No," answered Bill. "Not where I live."

The rifle Hart would not sell has a beautifully hand-bored, hand-rifled barrel, a mechanism with a double cock and double-set trigger and an ornately carved mountain mahogany stock. Bored to .45 caliber, the barrel is made of fine Swedish steel.

Accurately described by Buckskin as "a rotating helix driven by fingers on a headblock nailed to a tabletop," the machine used to make that rifle is not one whit more, and is primitive-looking at that. It scarcely seems sophisticated enough to un-cork a popgun, yet the rifle it produced shoots with deadly accuracy. "It's nothing but muscle power," Sylvan says, "but I really lay into it. That cutter comes out of there smoking."

Smoother than rosewood, the stock had been blackened with sulfuric acid and rubbed to its lustrous deep-brown finish with the palm of the hand. Its carvings depict the activities of mountain sheep.

"I just make one as I need it, but I don't like to spend less'n a year making a rifle," Hart said, opening the patch button in the stock to show the orange flicker feathers inside. These are used to flick dust and lint out of the mechanism.

Sylvan demonstrated how neatly the flint-tipped hammer struck the frizzen to create a spark, dropping it white-hot into a grain-of-wheat-sized charge of priming powder, and how the firing pin sloped just right to send the resulting fire into the main charge.

The red-striped ramrod is hickory specially cut in East Texas, and even the bright red and green tassels on the accompanying pouch have a specific, if whimsical, purpose. "They might just be decorations," says Buckskin, in one of his frequent indulgences in melodrama, "or you could tie one to a bush and a pursuer would want to fetch up to study on it."

For somewhat more ordinary purposes, the pouch is well equipped indeed. Priming horn, powder horn, "bosers," borers and cleaners, extra flints, rigs to chip flints, vent pickers and scrapers and even a bullet mold pour out of it in splendid profusion.

Following his regular ritual, Hart showed how he pours powder down the muzzle (30 grains), pushes in a bullet on a patch cut from a World War I bandage and tamps it down a bit with three different "bosers." After ramrodding the patch down to the powder, he tapped the rod lightly "to seat the bullet" and primed the firing pin. One could still see the shiny spot on the spherical lead bullet where the sprue had been filed off. "Oh, yes, I make my own bullets," Sylvan said. "That's simple, but I make my own bullet molds, too." Accompanying this arsenal is a stock of powder and bullets sufficient to fight an Indian war.

In the event of demand exhausting his supply of ammunition,

Buckskin could turn to his knives. Most formidable of these are a matched set of three of the most enormous bowie knives in or out of captivity, their guillotinelike blades suitably inscribed with such inspirational messages as "Liberty or Death," "Kill or Be Killed" and "Nuts." Hart also has classic daggers and French knives, but it is the bowies he likes best.

The tools with which Hart creates these masterworks and others are a cornucopia of finely tempered, ingenious instruments—hundreds of them—too specialized and original to have names. There are scrapers, gouges, skewed chisels, awls, adzes and fine-tolerance dies, taps and punches in sizes and shapes beyond counting. Also there are copperworking tools, silverworking tools, woodworking tools and blacksmithing tools. Beaten from such basic material as abandoned moonshine stills and mining machinery (with gold amalgam still sticking to it), even Hart's lowliest copper pot bears the imprint of his original design.

"My idea of art is to make sure you have good utensils—things you use every day—before you go fooling with pictures," Hart declares. "That's the Scandinavian idea, too." No Danish artisan should object to having his work compared with Hart's bowls, ladles, kettles, lanterns, candle holders, samovar, coffeepots, tea balls, griddles and skillets.

To find something to put into one of these pots for dinner, we strolled around Sylvan's garden, seeking what we might devour. Even in earliest summer, the choice was impressive. At various stations in the 10,000-square-foot plot—fertilized by, among other things, one buried deer, two bear heads and one cougar skeleton—Hart had planted asparagus, parsnips, carrots, beets, cabbage, corn, squash, cucumbers, cantaloupes, peppers, garlic, strawberries, horseradish, rhubarb, rutabaga, kohlrabi, kidney beans, purple beans, white potatoes, purple potatoes . . .

Purple potatoes? "Just like the Incas used to have," Buckskin explained, cutting one for my inspection. It was indeed a shiny purple. "The only thing that makes white potatoes taste good is that there's some good-looking young lady serving them to you."

In addition to domesticated flora and such in-between species as perpetual onion ("If you see those, you know the Hudson's Bay Company has been there. The company used to give, among other things, seed, eight pounds of flour and five of salt as board, and its traders had to grow or shoot the rest"), Hart plucks certain wild groceries for his table. An informal garden of Oregon grapes, squaw cabbage, dandelion, shadbush berries, currants, rose hips, gooseberries, brodiaea roots and oyster plant roots grows adjacent to the vegetables.

For that evening's meal, Hart selected beans, onions, asparagus, carrots, pieces of imported chuck roast, unidentified bones and chopped potatoes, all of which he put in a massive kettle rather similar to, though somewhat scaled down from, the variety generally used to parboil missionaries in comic strips. For those who might be wondering about it, purple potatoes, when boiled, turn a bright blue. Together with the bright green beans and bright orange carrots, the bright blue potatoes deserved immortalization in *Better Homes and Gardens.*

After eating this gourmet's delight plus some of Bill's preserved pears, we settled down comfortably to talk and to watch a candle wage its unequal struggle against gathering dusk. During a pause in our conversation I looked around the kitchen house. Of all the thousand articles, useful and whimsical, that inhabited its pegs and shelves, the boxes and boxes of tea caught my eye. Besides a native variety that Hart claims the Indians once picked, mint, Keemun, lapsang souchong, South American maté, gunpowder, jasmine, India, Russian, ningchow, Japan pan-fried, Irish, oolong, Darjeeling, Earl Grey's and English Breakfast teas marched in ranks and rows. The prize of the lot, labeled "Boston Harbour Tea, 'Bawstonaba' Registered, Blended and Packed by Davison Newman & Co. Ltd., 14 Creechurch Lane, London E.C. 3, The firm which supplied Tea 1773–1774 for the historic Boston Tea Parties," preserved on its sides a complete if microscopic copy of "The Petition of Davison & Newman to King George III claiming compensation for Chests of their Tea thrown into the harbour of Boston, Massachusetts, by Persons disguised as Indians."

"Is is true," I asked, "that you used to go to town for nothing but tea, books and powder?"

"When it's forty miles to town on ropes and snowshoes," said Buckskin dryly, "that's about all you can carry." His total supply of other imported goods, some $50 worth, was brought in on a neighbor's pack string once a year, in the autumn. Flour, sugar, coffee, oatmeal, rice and raisins were almost the sole freight. "One year, when I had been prospecting at Florence [another ghost gold town], I walked clear to Grangeville [96 miles from Five Mile] and brought back all my supplies myself," remembered Buckskin.

Later Sylvan showed me where he had lived when newly come to the Salmon in 1932, sleeping under a tree and doing his baking in a stone oven. The land was a placer mining claim then, and Hart bought 50 acres for one dollar. "You could have bought the whole Salmon River for ten thousand," he says.

One of Hart's favorite occupations in those early days was to take frequent long hikes to visit the still-living pioneers of the region, his purpose being to pick their brains for every grain of information about the fast-fading frontier life. Many of the pioneers became the young man's friends, notably Pres Wilson, whose ancestors had traded with Andrew Jackson; John Moore, "an honest moonshiner" who made his likker from apples; and old Henry Smith, who used to deliver mail for the area on snowshoes and left Buckskin his treasured rifle. But in that remote country, Sylvan says, "even if someone didn't like you very well he was still kind of glad to see you."

Polly Bemis, famed in legend as a bride won in a poker game, lived just ten miles downriver until 1933. Her real story is perhaps more interesting. Brought to Warren as a Chinese slave girl, she became a dance-hall hostess at the place where Charles Bemis was shot in a gunfight. Polly nursed Bemis back to health, and in gratitude he married her.

There were plenty of authentically rough characters left over from the times when there were 1,500 men at now silent Campbell's Ferry, and some carried about gold dust from the Thunder Mountain boom in quart jars.

People have always had a way of vanishing without a trace along the River of No Return. Old Campbell himself, owner of Campbell's Ferry, disappeared in a snowstorm one day and was never seen again. "Easiest country in the world to murder anyone," Hart says comfortably. "Suppose you go back East and marry someone and decide you don't want that kind of woman at all. Just bring her out here on a hunting trip and say she got lost. This is too big a country to search all of it."

The grand finale of one of Idaho's otherworldly sunsets now demanded our attention. It took me some time to see what made the sunset strangely beautiful: the air is so pellucidly clear that the sundown is never red, not even purple. There is simply not enough dust to diffract light sufficiently. Instead, tints of green, reflected from the dark forests, vary the turquoise, azure, ultramarine and purest blue of the sky. That latter blue is the poignant blue of Idaho's flowering camas prairies, and in its extraordinary depths one glimpses the very color of a pioneer woman's eyes, the very gingham of her frock.

Then it was full night. The candle flame shifted and flickered in a faint draft, rearranging the shadows. Its light now lit what appeared to be three skulls, resting in a recess over the fireplace, directly under a muzzle-loading rifle, a buffalo powder horn and a bullet mold. The death's heads on left and right were slit-eyed, fanged cougar skulls; that in the center, reposing on an ancient Greek Bible, looked all too human. This, it unfolded, was another "lost" Idahoan. Hart, who found the unholy relic washed up on the river edge, deduced that its previous owner, in life, had been a boy caught stealing provisions from early settlers, shot and thrown into the torrent.

"You see some fearful things in this country," Buckskin said. "I was up on Horse Heaven last June and I looked down in the canyon and saw a bolt of lightning begin and end below me. Some of those lightning bolts are a foot wide. If they hit a tree, the tree explodes. You see that for free. Sometimes ball lightning comes rolling down the hill, rivulets running down from it like molten gold. Saint Elmo's fire is common, and I once had some come down the stovepipe while a visitor was making coffee. I heard this screaming and yelling. 'It came right out of the coffeepot,' he said.

"Then there are places down on South Fork where you can find rows of pottery set just as the Indians left them. Lucky McKinnon found a cave with baskets, too. In a good dry cave those baskets could have set there 500 years."

Old Indian signs and art—which, self-taught, he has learned to read—also captivate Hart. His favorite story in that regard is of finding an ancient sign up South Fork just as the Idaho skies were preparing to open up and let loose. "At first I thought it was a trail marker," he recalls, "but it was a 'house' sign—meaning hogan, tepee, hotel. There was nothing there but a straight, sheer cliff, but I spread my bedroll anyway. Well, the drip from that pouring rain missed me by just *this* much all night. A message from a thousand to five thousand years ago had kept me dry.

"Five Mile Bar is the only place on the river with good firewood," he said, changing subjects. "That's because there's never been a woman here. A woman sets around the stove all day burning fuel." Besides, Buckskin implies, he doesn't regard too kindly some of the women he does see. "I was taking a little bath in the river one day when I heard all this hollering and screaming," he relates. "I had just had time to get on my long red underwear and these women came round the bend yelling that their rubber boat was leaking. I hauled them out, prob'ly saved their lives, and all the while those frozen-faced women were sitting there looking disapproving. Well, first, I had less hide showing than they did, and then I don't think they were showing any proper appreciation a'tall.

"I've got six months, from November on, when this place is just like it's always been," Hart said. "Nobody visits, and I get mail twice a month. If I want to go anywhere, I put a pack on my back, get my gun, take off and stay as little or as long as I like. What more could you want?

"For the city man, life is just a jumble, like the facts in a college freshman's notebook. But you can ask me anything about nearly anything and I can answer, because I've had time to think about it."

Every word—and every copper pot—had been a tacit answer to the basic question: Why had he come here in the first place? But now Bill answered it direct.

"It is," said Buckskin slowly but readily, "a custom of my family, going back about 300 years, for the young men to stay in the woods for a year. Edward Hart, father of John Hart, who signed the Declaration of Independence, did it, moving from Connecticut to then-wild Mercer County, New Jersey. The next John Hart was one of the first Kansans, and my father went to Creek county of Oklahoma. I just liked it so well I never came out."

It was quite possible to believe it was as simple and extraordinary as that—a man living as he was just because he liked that life. "But I wouldn't want to waste any time in complaining about what passes for civilization," Sylvan was demurring. "That's too negative. You should be able to see what's wrong about it with just a side glance, that's all.

"The good things a person needs—stubbornness, thinking for himself—don't make him a 'useful member of society.' What-makes him 'useful' is to be half-dead. On weekends they open all the cemeteries and all those dead people march out. All the same sickly shade of hide, all sunken-eyed, not really seeing anything, just walking about because it's a weekend. Like I say, dead people. Then Monday—well, they don't all go back to the cemetery, where they belong. They ought to be honor-bound to go back where they'd be happier, the poor human ciphers lead such pitiful circumscribed lives."

It was late and we prepared for bed. The moon was not yet risen, but starlight poured down into the canyon, turning the granite opposite wall a chalk white etched with black, black pines. Where the stars are not shut out by the visual pollution of mercury vapor lamps—that blue glare fit only to light concentration camps—the eye can see again. At Five Mile Bar it can see a dark, mighty river under a pristine sky.

Such purity is rare in a night now, and, settling into my sleeping bag on one of Sylvan Hart's comfortable improvised beds, I watched the black-green Salmon hurry down to the Snake and saw Sylvan's collection of skulls phosphoresce softly in the half-light.

AN ISLAND TO MYSELF

Tom Neale

In his youth an ordinary seaman, and for years a shopkeeper among
the Cook Islands, New Zealander Tom Neale was in his fifties when he
turned his back on society and went into his lonely retreat on a South
Pacific atoll named Suvarov. It had been used by the New Zealand
"coastwatchers" during World War II to spy on Japanese naval and
aerial movements. The atoll had a broken-down shack, some cooking
equipment—skimpy things left by the coastwatchers when they returned to New Zealand after the war—and this was where Tom Neale
went as a sudden hermit, to live a Thoreauesque life. He sets the scene
for us as follows:

This is the story of more than five years spent alone, in two spells,
on an uninhabited coral atoll half a mile long and three hundred yards
wide in the South Pacific. It was two hundred miles from the nearest
inhabited island, and I first arrived there on October 7, 1952, and
remained alone (with only two yachts calling) until June 24, 1954,
when I was taken off ill after a dramatic rescue.

I was unable to return to the atoll until April 23, 1960, and this time
I remained alone until December 27, 1963.

Tom Neale
Tahiti and Rarotonga, 1964–1965

I was fifty when I went to live alone on Suvarov, after thirty
years of roaming the Pacific, and in this story I will try to de-

scribe my feelings, try to put into words what was, for me, the most remarkable and worthwhile experience of my whole life.

I chose to live in the Pacific islands because life there moves at the sort of pace which you feel God must have had in mind originally when He made the sun to keep us warm and provided the fruits of the earth for the taking; but though I came to know most of the islands, for the life of me I sometimes wonder what it was in my blood that had brought me to live among them. There was no history of wanderlust in my family that I knew of—other than the enterprise which had brought my father, who was born in Aylesbury, Buckinghamshire, out to New Zealand after serving with the 17th Lancers. By the time he met my mother, who came of sound pioneering stock, he had become a company secretary. And so I was born in Wellington, though while I was still a baby we moved to Greymouth in New Zealand's South Island, where my father was appointed paymaster to the state coal mines. Here we remained until I was about seven, when the family—I had two brothers and three sisters—moved to Timaru on the opposite side of South Island. . . .

Looking back, I imagine the real clue to my future aspirations lay in the fact that it always seemed absolutely natural that I should go to sea. I cannot remember ever contemplating any other way of life and there was no opposition from my parents when I announced I would like to join the New Zealand Navy. My real ambition was to become a skilled navigator, but when my father took me to Auckland Naval Base to sign on, I was dismayed to discover that already I was too old at eighteen and a half to be apprenticed as a seaman. . . .

I spent four years in the New Zealand Navy before buying myself out, and I left only because of a nagging desire to see more of the world than the brief glimpses we obtained beyond the confining, narrow streets of the ports where we docked. And our visits were dictated by naval necessity—simple things like routine patrols or defective boilers—so that I saw Papeete but never Tahiti; Apia but never Samoa; Nukualofa but never Tonga. It was the islands I always longed to see, not a vista of dock cranes or the sleazy bars which one can find in every maritime corner of the world.

For the next few years I wandered from island to island. Sometimes I would take a job for a few months as fireman on one of the slow, old, interisland tramps. When I tired of this, I would settle down for a spell, clearing bush or planting bananas. There was always work, and there was always food. And it was only now that I really came to know and love the islands strung like pearls across the South Pacific—Manihiki at dawn as the schooner threads its way through the pass in the reef; Papeete at sunset with the Pacific lapping up against the main street; the haze on the coconut palms of Puka-Puka; the clouds above Mooréa with its jagged silhouette of extinct volcanoes; Pago Pago where Somerset Maugham created the character of Sadie Thompson, and where you can still find the Rainmaker's Hotel; Apia where Aggie Grey's Hotel welcomes guests with a large whisky and soda, and where (so I was told later) Michener was inspired to create Bloody Mary. . . .

I knew all the islands and atolls, as a wanderer and sailor. I had seen Suvarov on one of my trips—the atoll of the former "coastwatchers." What I saw pleased me. I would settle down on Suvarov alone. In 1952 my opportunity came. Dick Brown, an independent trader in Rarotonga, where I worked for years, had gone into the shipping business after the war, buying a long, narrow submarine chaser of less than a hundred tons, which he had converted into an interisland trader. She was called the *Mahurangi,* and quite by chance I heard that on her next trip she was going north to Palmerston Island and then to Manihiki. I did not need a map to know that the course passed right by Suvarov.

In all my years in the Cooks, I had never heard of a trading vessel sailing this direct route; it was an opportunity which might never come my way again.

I totted up my finances. I had saved 79 Pounds. I went to Dick and asked when he was sailing.

"In two weeks," he replied.

"How much would it cost to divert on the way to Manihiki and take me to Suvarov?"

He scratched his head, figuring.

"Thirty quid."

It seemed a lot of money, especially when the *Mahurangi* must pass almost within sight of Suvarov and could have dropped me off with little trouble. But diverting a vessel is always expensive and I did not argue.

"Done!" I said, and we shook hands on it.

I had just two weeks to gather together everything I thought a man would need to survive on an uninhabited coral atoll. Two weeks—and 49 Pounds. . . .

How well I remember my very first purchase. It was a sack of Australian flour, from a shipment which had just arrived. This was a rare luxury in Raro as we naturally bought everything we could from New Zealand, but I had cooked with Australian flour from time to time and knew from experience that it would keep much longer than the local brand.

I also knew that once the news of its arrival got around, there would be a run on it, for the South Seas stores are really more like warehouses than shops, and when shipments of new lines arrive to be piled up against the shelves of the barnlike buildings, everyone in town rushes to buy. So I was down at Raro's "shopping district" as soon as the stores opened, asking the assistant at Donald's, whom I had known for years, "Any of the Australian flour left?"

"Sure, Tom," he replied. "How much—a couple of pounds?"

"How much is it?"

"Sixpence a pound."

"Oh, well"—I pretended to hesitate, secretly enjoying the joke—"might as well take a fifty-pound sack!"

He nearly dropped it; and at that moment the wife and

daughter of a government official came in, and stared in astonishment at the sight of Neale buying a whole sack of flour, so on the spur of the moment I added, as casually as I could, "While I'm here, I'd better take a seventy-pound bag of sugar!"

After that, the news was soon round Raro—even though I said very little myself. But you can't keep secrets on an island of only 8000 people, especially when I—normally so careful—began to buy goods by the sackful. . . .

I even had more than one proposition from the ladies. And I may say that I was tempted, for the Cook Island women are not only handsome but wonderfully adaptable, used to hard work, and can turn their hands to anything. Frisbie had found great happiness with his native wife, so when one woman of about 30, the sister of a Cook Island friend, quite seriously offered to come (adding ingenuously, "You don't need to marry me!"), I definitely considered the possibility. I decided against it. . . .

I was, however, worried about the possibility of a toothache, for that was something I could not control. I had had an upper plate for several years, but I went to the dentist and told him to take out as many of my bottom teeth as he wanted! It says much for my simple life that he extracted only one—and I have never had toothache.

I had to take some medical precautions, but I could not afford to take a really extensive kit, much as I would have liked to have it. Drugs cost so much. So I had to content myself with plenty of bandages, sticking plaster, Germolene, a supply of Band-Aid, a little cotton wool, one bottle of Vaseline, and a half-pint bottle of Merthiolate, plenty of antiseptic, some sulphur thiazol (M & B) tablets for fevers. I bought no aspirin because I never get headaches.

Of course, I did not spend one day buying food, or another selecting pots and pans. Like any housewife, I became a familiar figure in the local stores, carrying my shopping lists, and buying whatever I needed from the heaped shelves and counters. I used to stagger home with my purchases, tick them off on my list, and then pack them in a motley assembly of variously sized parcels, making a note of the contents of each packet. . . .

Tobacco was a real luxury. I don't smoke a great deal, but one cigarette has always seemed to go with that evening cup of tea I love so much. I bought half a pound of tobacco and a dozen packets of cigarette papers.

At first I was unable to decide whether or not to take a shotgun. I had heard rumors that the coastwatchers had left some pigs on the island, which would be quite wild by now, perhaps savage. And, too, I knew there were plenty of birds on Suvarov. But there were several reasons against taking a gun. I don't *like* killing living things; nor could I really afford a gun. . . .

While accumulating all this gear, I was also busy buying seeds for the garden I knew I would have to make. I bought packets of tomatoes, cucumbers, rock melon (known in Europe as canteloupes), watermelon, runner beans, and Indian spinach, which trails along the ground with thicker, fleshier leaves than ordinary spinach.

I also purchased some shallots, a few tubers of sweet potatoes or yams—known in the Cooks as kumeras, an old Maori word —that I knew would quickly send up shoots which could be pulled out and planted. Finally, I bought two banana shoots in case the banana trees on the island had been torn down by a hurricane. . . .

With the last of my money I went in search of my greatest luxury—a few books. Two days before the sailing date, I spent a morning browsing among the paperbacks on sale along Main Road. I already had a few books by Defoe, Stevenson, and other favorite authors. Frisbie's *Island of Desire* was certainly amongst them, but when it came to spending my last few shillings on reading matter, my choice was dictated by the stocks I could inspect. I knew that the coastwatchers had left some books on the island, but I had no certainty that they would please my taste. I *had* to take a few of my own choice—not many, for I derive great pleasure from rereading the same book (so long as I like it), but I was able to pick up three books by Somerset Maugham, two by Dickens (including *Oliver Twist*), *Mutiny on the Bounty* by Nordhoff and Hall (whom I had met on occasion), and several rather poor quality Westerns and Edgar Wallace thrillers, which featured predominantly on the local bookshelves.

On the last night but one, when I was riding my bicycle to the friend who had promised to keep it for me, I stopped by a small general store and picked up a book which was to give me great pleasure in the months ahead. Indeed, I must have read it a score of times. It was a dog-eared, secondhand copy of *Lord Jim*. . . .

My landing was hardly spectacular. Not far off the old wrecked pier the crew lowered a ship's boat, loaded my belongings aboard, and rowed me ashore. As the *Mahurangi*'s skipper had decided to stay in the lagoon until the following morning, my boat was followed by the passengers anxious for the chance to stretch their legs. So I came ashore in crowded company and almost before my crates and stores had been offloaded, the beach was busy with women washing clothes whilst the men hurried off to fish.

Quite suddenly, though still in the company of human beings, I felt a momentary pang of loneliness. Everybody seemed so busy that nobody had any time to notice me. The crew was already rowing back to the *Mahurangi;* the laughing, brown women were sorting out their washing; the fishermen had disappeared, while I stood, feeling a little forlorn, on the hot white beach under a blazing sun, surrounded by a mound of crates, parcels, and black stones, unceremoniously dumped near the pier. A plaintive miaow reminded me I had a friend. Mrs. Thievery was impatiently demanding her freedom. Leaving all my packages on the beach, except my Gladstone and the box with the two cats, I walked almost apprehensively the 50 yards up the coral path to the shack. . . .

Suddenly the shack was there in front of me and I must admit my heart sank. I had forgotten the amazing violence of tropical growth; forgotten, too, just how long ago it was since men had lived here. Subconsciously I had always remembered Suvarov when the shack had been inhabited. And now, standing there with my bag and box at my feet, I could hardly distinguish the galvanized iron roof through the thick, lush creepers covering it. The outbuildings, too, seemed almost strangled beneath a profusion of growth. Cautiously I stepped onto the veranda which ran the length of the shack. The floor boards felt firm, but when I looked up at the roof, I saw the plaited coconut fronds had rotted away. And then, at one end of the veranda, I spotted the boat, upside down—with two quarter-inch cracks running right along her bottom. I knew immediately she would sink like a stone in the water; nor was this realization made any less depressing by the knowledge I had brought no calking with me.

It was all rather overpowering. I sat in the hot sun, mopped my brow, and opened up my faithful Gladstone bag and took out the screwdriver which I had packed on top of my clothes in order to be able to unscrew the netted top of the box and release the cats. In a moment the mother had jumped out, looking around her, and I set the kitten down alongside. Unlike me, they did not seem a bit deterred and proceeded to make themselves at home immediately. Within five minutes Mrs. Thievery had killed her first island rat.

I rolled myself a cigarette, sat on the veranda for a few moments, and looked around at the scene I remembered so well from my one brief visit. . . .

Round the back of the shack were the two water tanks, which I remembered. They were in good condition. One, built of circular corrugated iron, held about 300 gallons; the other, a square galvanized tank, held some 400 gallons. And when I turned on the taps, excellent water came gushing out. To my relief, this was quite drinkable. The tanks must have been well built and, since they rested on a wooden platform 18 inches above the ground, did not seem to have suffered the general process of decay. Fed from the guttering along the wall, each was almost full.

Behind the shack I discovered a latrine some eight feet deep, situated some little distance away. This handy convenience was lined with two oil drums whose bottoms had been thoughtfully knocked out. On the spur of the moment, I christened it "The House of Meditation.". . .

Some 15-foot miki-miki trees were growing almost out of the bare rock at the water's edge, and I made a mental note about them; I would find their hard branches invaluable, for they make the best sticks in the world for husking coconuts. A few yards farther on I spied some young pawpaws 50 yards inland and decided to give them a closer look. I had almost reached them when a violent flurry in the undergrowth scared the wits out of me. Almost before I realized what had happened, I had a glimpse of a wild pig lumbering away with astonishing speed. But my momentary fear quickly gave way to anger when I realized I had disturbed the brute in the very act of tearing out the green young shoots of some pawpaw—one of the fruits on which I would have to depend. Those pigs presented a real problem. . . .

There was a natural bathing pool and the water was blue, clear, and enticing. Pylades Bay would certainly be my private swimming pool. Behind it, the ground was covered with hibiscus trees and densely matted tauhuna, and from the beach I could see several uprooted coconut trees, the long, slender, dead-straight trunks lying just where they had crashed. I remembered Frisbie telling me, "The most awesome thing in the hurricane was watching, actually watching, the wind take an old coconut tree eighty feet tall and tear it out of the ground. . . ."

I was immensely happy during those first few days. Before starting to unpack everything, I cleaned out the shack thoroughly, scrubbing the floors and washing down the walls. Then I spent three or four days hard at work tearing down the creepers and vines from the roof of the shack and hacking them away from the shed with my machete. I finished plaiting the veranda roof and had to nail up two of the shutters which had become loose. There seemed no end to the work, but before long I had made a shelf in the bathhouse and then I fixed up a clothesline between two hibiscus trees at the bottom of the yard, high enough to hang out my bed linen.

All this took a long time for I had to fish for the cats (and myself!) and though I did very little cooking at first, I had to make a fire and this meant collecting firewood from all over the island. But I was determined to clean up the place before I did anything else, and only when this was done did I set about sorting out my supplies. . . .

After work, I would catch some fish in the early evening, cook it, and then, if the weather was fine, take a bowl of tea down to the beach and sit there on a box-chair which I had made so I could watch the sun go down—one of my favorite pastimes.

Then I would explore something very different from my daytime activities—the books left by the coastwatchers. These were a mixed bag, I must admit, and if I describe my own taste in literature as catholic, I don't know what denomination to use in describing theirs!

I decided that half of them were not worth reading at all—a decision I reversed after a year when I was only too glad to read *anything*. But there were some gems among the trash, including several books of which I had never heard.

One evening I picked up *Brave New World* by Aldous Huxley. I remember I was very tired that night, and meant to read only a few pages to lull me to sleep. I was kept awake half the night, entranced by a description of a world so horrifying that time after time I would stop, reflect on what I had read, and say, "Neale—if *that's* what the world is going to be like, you just stay where you are!" Even the crowing of the cock failed to wake me that morning!

During the first weeks the problems of settling in occupied most of my time, but I did make a tentative start on some of the more long-term projects I had in mind.

Though the prospect of eggs for breakfast seemed remote, I tried to cajole the fowls by scattering grated coconut at the far end of the yard. I had plans to tame them and collect them all into one run and after the first couple of weeks I noticed they were a lot less hesitant about approaching the shack. . . .

My basic diet, however, still continued to be fish, particularly as I was hoarding my "special" supplies like a miser; I suppose instinctively I was guarding against a rainy day—literally a rainy day—when fishing might be impossible, or I could be confined to my shack.

Sometimes I would eat one of the coconut crabs which I found in small numbers on Suvarov. But I never really cared for them. They were ugly, brutal creatures, at least a foot long, with a pair of claws strong enough to crush a finger. Some of the islanders I had known considered their tails a great delicacy, but I found them too rich. Besides, coconut crabs are scavengers which will eat anything. They would have eaten me had I died! I roasted one occasionally when I really felt a need for a change of diet. Their claws were good, but my dislike for these repugnant creatures tended to spoil my appetite, so that when the cats and I got heartily sick of ku or raw parrot fish, and were desperate for a change of flavor, I preferred to go after larger fish. . . .

Every fish in the lagoon seemed to queue up for my table (except, curiously, turtles, which were rare). Perhaps the easiest to catch was the reef cod, which lay motionless in the pools as I approached. They never even moved until my spear was within six inches of them, and once I had them quivering on shore, I carried them back to the shack and steamed them in saltwater in my aluminum pan over a fire beneath a piece of flattened old iron roofing.

Early in January the first heavy rains drenched the island. Three months of backbreaking work lay behind me, but now at last I could begin to see some results, for I had settled down to a happy, easy, solitary—but never lonely—life. I kept my shack spotlessly clean; I had built a small lean-to on the beach, roofing it with plaited pandanus (which lasts much longer than a coconut roof), and here I sipped my evening cup of tea at the end of each day's toil. If I could not chalk up a success in my efforts to tame the fowls, at least I felt they were slowly becoming more friendly, lured on when I started offering them tern eggs. I had also begun to make a garden fence, and I had sown my seeds in shallow boxes. The breadfruit tree was flourishing; so were the two banana shoots in their squares of coconut logs. Even the cats seemed to be more contented than ordinary cats, and when the barometer started to tumble, warning me of bad weather on the way, I buried my tool chest in its safety hole, and was able to reflect, almost placidly, that I had enough dry wood to keep a fire going for six months.

I had made careful preparations against bad weather. Two weeks' supply of uto was already cooked and in its special box. I still had plenty of bully beef, coffee, tea, sugar, and a fair supply of flour—though it was going a bit wormy, and I had to sieve it through the invaluable tea strainer. In truth, I had been awaiting the rain almost with impatience, not because we needed rain (for Suvarov is blessed with regular, short, sharp tropical storms), but for an entirely different and almost comical reason. Bad weather would give me my first holiday! . . .

For over two weeks heavy rain lashed the island, while high winds tore shrieking through the trees, and coconuts rattled on the tin roof of my shack. There was never any serious danger of hurricanes that winter, but even though I was snugly protected from the rain, nothing—not even the shield of the low jungle—could keep out what Frisbie described as "the ungodly roar" of the wind, or the twang as it sang through the taut guy ropes, which shuddered each time the shack trembled.

At times the wind was so fierce that when I ventured outside, the torrents seemed to be driven almost horizontally. At night, particularly, I could actually see the rain through the frenzied tops of the smaller coconut trees, and it was hard to believe that all this water whipping past came from the heavens, for it was almost parallel to the ground, as though it spurted from some distant hose pipe with a gigantic spray. . . .

Suvarov was an island capable of constant surprises. One day I came across a patch of arrowroot growing wild. It was the sort the islanders prize, since it makes better starch than any of the packets you can buy in stores. When I dug it out, I found it had a bulbous root which went nine inches down into the sand. Out of this root sprouted pale green hollow stems, with leaves rather similar to those of a pawpaw. The leaf withers when the plant matures, and this is the right moment to dig out the bulb. The ones I found on Suvarov varied enormously in size. Some were the size of small apples, whilst others weighed up to three pounds. I used this arrowroot to make poi, a very popular native dish in the South Seas. At first I mixed it with pawpaw, though later, when the garden was producing, I was to vary this with bananas or pumpkins.

It was quite a business, preparing this dish. After washing the bulbs I grated them, and then came the big operation. Earlier, I had put four pegs in the ground, not too far apart, and each about two feet high. Over these I had stretched a bit of sheeting and placed my washbasin beneath it.

On top of this sheet I piled the grated arrowroot and then poured cold water over it, stirring it with my hand until the water strained through. At first the water which drained into the bowl was milky, but with each subsequent can of water it became increasingly clear so that I knew all the starch must have been washed into the bowl, leaving on the sheet only a remainder of fiber, which I threw away. When I picked up the bowl, the starch had sunk to the bottom. I poured the water off, then put the intensely white, very fine starch into the sun to dry. . . .

"Neale," I told myself firmly one day, "what you need now is a boat."

Would the old tub stand the strain? I decided it was worth a try. Quite aside from the fact that if I got her afloat I would be able to ferry loads of soil for the garden, I knew that, once she was seaworthy, I could sail to Motu Tou, six miles across the lagoon, or to any other of the small islets in the 50 square miles of water inside the reef.

I looked her over carefully. Frankly, she was not impressive —ten feet long and three feet wide, a most ungainly, flat-bottomed craft. Her sides were in fairly good shape, but her keel of three-inch-thick 12-inch-long planks showed gaping quarter-inch cracks between each pair of planks.

However was I going to calk her? What a fool I had been not to bring some oakum! I suddenly remembered a length of two-inch-thick rope which I had found after the *Mahurangi* sailed and had stored in the shed. Getting it out, I found it to be about 15 feet long, and I cut it into yard-long pieces, which I teased strand by strand until I had something which resembled a supply of oakum. I made a rough paintbrush with another bit of old rope and got to work on the ruin. Working on the veranda, I doused the open seams with plenty of green paint and then calked them with my homemade oakum, taking care not to drive it in too hard, since that would have been fatal at this stage. . . .

I must have done a really good job, for once I launched her, she never leaked, and once I was satisfied she was seaworthy, I named her, in red paint on her stern, the *Ruptured Duckling* in memory of an old friend in Tahiti whose canoe had borne the same name.

The *Ruptured Duckling,* ungainly and difficult though she was, proved invaluable; and soon I was towing her through the shallows to the south end of the island where I would spend a day gathering soil. I could haul a full load back in an hour or two—a load which would have taken me days to carry on my back. . . .

During these weeks I had come a long way toward taming a duck. She would allow me within five paces of her—maybe because she had become so dependent on her evening meal.

"The wild duck is making herself at home all right," I wrote. "I still put grated coconut in a tin and a tin of water alongside. She takes a mouthful of nut, then dips her bill in the water— does it with every mouthful. Her wing feathers look a bit the worse for wear, so I expect she's not young. She spends the greater part of her day in the shade, standing on one leg, with her head thrown back sleeping, but with one eye open; then disappears just before sunset. Mr. Tom Tom [the kitten] has stalked her a couple of times. I've had to speak to him sharply about that."

I often wondered where she spent the night. I had never seen her fly away, but one evening I had just left the bathhouse when I noticed her waddling toward the lagoon. Instinctively I sensed she had some definite purpose. I stood and watched.

As soon as she had reached the edge of the clearing where the ground sloped down to the lagoon, she took off, flying low—a few feet only above the ground—between the coconut trees toward the beach. From then on she changed course, heading out over the lagoon and making for Whale Islet, three-quarters of a mile away. A few evenings later I saw her do the same thing again—and she never varied this habit, but flew precisely the same course through the trees and over the water. . . .

On August 4, 1953—ten months after I had landed—I welcomed my first visitors. . . .

There, in the shimmering distance, was a sail. I stared in momentary disbelief, but there it was, one of the most beautiful sights the Pacific can ever offer—a ship in full sail edging her way through the blue waters. She was plainly making for the entrance to the lagoon. It was so long since I had seen a sail that it took an appreciable time for the reality to sink in, for me to realize that in an hour or two, I would actually be talking to other people; men, perhaps women; talking to them, instead of to myself! . . .

Before I reached the shack, the vessel had lowered her sail and was entering the passage under auxiliary power. I hurried inside to change my strip of pareu for a pair of shorts in case there were ladies aboard.

By the time I had come out again, the boat had dropped anchor in 30 feet of water about a hundred yards off the old pier, and I remember how another thought suddenly struck me that the pier which had been smashed up in the 1942 hurricane was an eyesore, and it was high time I tidied it up. . . .

As I pushed the *Duckling* off the beach and into the water, I could see four people crowding the rails of the yacht. They waved, but of course as soon as I began rowing across the lagoon my back was turned toward them, so I did not really see them until a few moments later when I came alongside, and two men were helping me to make fast the dinghy whilst two women looked on. Then I was aboard—and within a few minutes was drinking tea brewed by somebody else for the first time in ten months. And with milk in it!

The elder of the two men held out a hand. "My name's Tom Worth." He was approaching middle age, looked very fit, without a spare ounce of flesh.

"And I'm Mrs. Worth," said a slender lady, who looked very pleasant.

"I'm Tom Neale," I replied, wondering whether Dr. Livingstone had felt as tongue-tied when Stanley introduced himself, for I had often pictured this precise moment—the exact moment of meeting strangers—and I had contemplated it with a certain nervousness. After all, what could one say to strangers? Especially as they would probably regard me with the suspicion normally reserved for a mental case.

There was a moment of almost embarrassed silence and then Tom Worth said something that staggered me—and broke the ice.

"Oh, yes!" he laughed cheerfully. "We all know all about

you!" He turned to his two younger passengers, and introduced them as Mr. and Mrs. Taylor.

Whilst Mrs. Worth poured the tea, I asked how they had come to find out about my being here. "The British Consul in Tahiti told me," Tom Worth explained. "I believe he's an old friend of yours. You know what he said? 'Call in at Suvarov and see whether or not Tom Neale has kicked what remains of the island into the sea with those big boots of his.' ". . .

The following morning, they all rowed ashore for a last bath and, as I recorded in my journal, "I gave them some more spring onions, eggs, melons, fish, which they said they appreciated very much. They gave me some tea, sugar, a jar of Scotch black-currant jelly, and a little flour."

And then just before the *Beyond* sailed, with a strong southeasterly wind to blow her on her way, Tom Worth came back to the shack with a final gift—a bottle of rum.

This touched me very much, and as the *Beyond* sailed out toward the pass, I did in actual fact experience a queer feeling of loss. I remember thinking, too, how vastly different their lives were going to be from mine once their pleasant cruise was over. Even when they reached Apia in Samoa, there would be bright lights (of a sort), cars, busy streets, cinemas, hotels; so-called luxuries which, however desirable, exacted their own price in tensions, problems, congested humanity.

It was a price I had long ago decided I was not interested in paying. So I stood by the edge of the old pier watching their sail disappear round the end of the island from whence they would head for the channel and the open sea. It would soon be dusk, the end of another, but this time an unusual, day on my island. So unusual that I watched for a little longer because this had been a happy time. But once the *Beyond* was through the pass and heading out to sea, I turned my back on the lagoon and strode up the coral path to the shack.

The first thing I did was take off my shorts and put on my strip of pareu again.

I was struck down with fever. This proved to be the worst bout so far, and came just at a moment when my resistance was at its lowest. I had been depressed before, but this seemed the final straw. The symptoms were unmistakable—chattering teeth, hot flushes (so that I never really knew whether I was hot or cold), and the feeling that my legs were going to buckle under me.

I managed to gather a few drinking nuts around my bed and lay down to sweat it out for 36 hours. Maybe it was lucky I had no idea the bout was going to last for nearly four days.

I hate now to think of the dizzy heights to which my temperature must have soared. Yet the curious thing is that I can remember almost every detail of those four days—and those four never-ending nights.

The fever engulfed me in waves, and looking back, I always associate it with the pounding on the reef and the pier. I suppose it was the only sound I could hear as I unwillingly hovered between moments when my brain was clear and that other semidelirious dreamworld which always seemed to be reaching out for me. Each time I felt myself slipping down there, I struggled to hold on to the real world, and as I struggled, the pounding in my head (or out on the reef) would increase, so that it began to seem, in a way, like drowning.

I can remember those fits of fever now (or so I like to think) with a curious, crystal clarity. I can remember being suddenly afraid, at the height of one bout, that I had forgotten to bury my cache of tools, and managing to struggle out of bed and walk shakily toward the door. (But I begin to wonder now if I really did this, or if it was only a dream so vivid that I really believed it happened.)

I was well enough, soon enough, four days later.

I celebrated Christmas Day with an outsized turtle steak—it seemed the finest meat dish I had ever tasted—and because I was afraid the rest would go bad, I cut it up into chunks and stewed it with some spring onions. After this feast, I decided to keep my last tin of bully beef for New Year's Eve—by which time I reckoned the turtle would be finished.

I was only just in time. Twenty-four hours after Christmas the barometer started falling with alarming speed. Though the next morning dawned perfectly calm, the flat, still sea was the color of lead, and Anchorage was blanketed by a stifling, suffocating heat. Nothing moved—not a palm frond, not a spiky pandanus leaf—and when I walked over to the east coast and looked out from Pylades Bay to the sea beyond the reef, even its calm held the hidden menace of a disguise, as though it were hoping to trap the unwary by its seemingly placid surface.

I knew the portents only too well (that trite old phrase about the calm before the storm) and strode back to the shack. There was no immediate hurry—but equally there was no doubt that serious trouble was on the way. Before doing anything else I checked my survival cache for tools, making sure my extra matches in their sealed tin were dry, and then took the box over to the burial hole in the outhouse. Next I lit a good fire on my brick hearth, and while it was burning, went out with my spear for a concentrated hour of fishing. It seemed provident to lay in some emergency rations, for there was no telling with a big storm; it could last a few hours or a few days.

I had plenty of cooked uto, but I foraged around for a couple of dozen more, which I cooked, and then I laid out double rations for the fowls. Next—as the first puffs of wind ruffled the palms—I inspected the garden for any ripe fruit which would be mercilessly blown off the plants when the inevitable storm broke.

By noon the calm had given way to the white horses that caused Conrad to write that the whole sea resembled "a floor of foaming crests," and the palm fronds were no longer still. The first winds had reached Anchorage, after traveling hundreds of miles from some great storm far away to the north. By the time I had tested the wire guy ropes lashing down my shack, I felt there was nothing more I could do in the way of preparation. . . .

By midafternoon gigantic seas were visible breaking all along the reef to the north, and before sunset, when the storm was beginning to reach its height, seas more huge than I had ever seen began breaking right across the half-mile width of the entrance to the passage. The rolling mass of water surged on through and over the passage, only gradually spending its massive force as it lost impetus in the great stretch of water inside the lagoon. I remember saying to myself, "Neale! This could be another 'forty-two."

The wind had risen in tremendous force, and the last thing I did outside before seeking the sanctuary of my shack was to struggle a couple of hundred yards to the highest point of the island. This was only 15 feet above normal sea level, but already from my vantage point it seemed as though Anchorage was beginning to shrink as waves came rolling through the gap in the barrier reef to engulf the beaches and creep up more and more greedily every minute. Just behind the beach and not far from the pier the first coconut tree fell with a crash, torn out by the roots, as though giant fingers were already starting to loot the island. Waves pounded right over the pier and, as I looked north, I could see more gigantic waves tearing through the half-mile stretch of fringing reef separating Anchorage from Whale Inlet, surging into the lagoon, now rapidly becoming an immense waste of boiling seas. . . .

Next morning I awoke to discover the sun bursting through the palms just as though nothing eventful had happened. It felt good to be alive. I must have slept late, for the cats were demanding food. . . .

I surveyed my atoll after the storm. My pier was gone. Six months of backbreaking labor had vanished overnight. The massive blocks which had torn my hands and fingers and brought me so much fever had been hurled back in chaos toward the beach, and now lay more or less all jumbled up where I had found them. . . .

"I was so downhearted," I wrote in my journal, "that I didn't even use bad language, but walked slowly back to the house."

Tom Neale, some months later, almost broke his back and was incapacitated for days. Four days later, fortunately, the American yacht Mandalay *came by—and two Americans, Bob Grant and James Rockefeller, from Maine, nursed Neale back to some sort of health. Eventually he was brought back to Rarotonga, to spend six more years at his old job. In 1960 Neale was back in Suvarov, rebuilding again. There had been some callers during his absence. On entering his shack, he discovered something:*

I picked up the white paper. It was a note dated March, 1956, and it read: "Don't know who you are or if you're returning, but would like you to know that my boat stayed here for two weeks. We enjoyed the fruits of your garden and ate five of your fowl. Hope this will cover everything. Sincerely, Sid Thatcher, San Francisco."

The other "bit of paper" was a $20 bill.

What a pleasant gesture from the unknown Mr. Thatcher! It conjured up all sorts of thoughts. Was there a Mrs. T? Were they still alive? I kept that bill for a long, long time—until one day when it came in very handy.

Between his idyllic solitary periods, Tom Neale had two visitors who arrived in two helicopters. Stunned when he saw them land, he raised his battered hat and said, "United States Navy, I presume?" They belonged to the American icebreaker Glacier, *on its way to the Antarctic via New Zealand. They left a half-hour later, sorry not to have brought cigarettes, whiskey and goodies along.*

There were other visitors, especially the Vessey family, also American, who came by in a 40-footer, the Tiburon. *When a storm tore the boat from its moorings and wrecked it on the coral reef, the Vessey family became the first castaways on Suvarov. Some months later, after bequeathing to Tom the salvaged working electrical equipment —to light up Neale's shack—they were picked up by the New Zealand frigate Pukaki. After that, Tom Neale returned to his hermit life.*

My second stay on Suvarov lasted about three and a half years, and during this time only six yachts called at the island; once 14 months passed without my seeing another human being; yet I was never lonely.

The first weeks were to set a pattern of living that lasted my entire time on the island. Never again did I punish myself with long hours of physical work as I had done during my first stay. I had learned a bitter lesson then—that you cannot overwork on an island diet—and I vowed never to forget it.

Now that I had had six years to relive every moment I had spent on the island, and to reflect on the mistakes I had made, I rather ruefully came to the conclusion that I, who loved the leisurely pace of life on the islands, had failed when I reached Suvarov the first time to put into practice the lessons learned during half a lifetime in the South Pacific. I could understand how it had happened. I had been so proud of my island that I wanted to do everything in a rush. And so, in a curiously ironic way, I had unwittingly imposed on the timeless quality of the island the speed and bustle of modern cities from which I had been so anxious to escape.

Perhaps this sounds a little exaggerated, but now that I was back, I was determined not to make the same mistake again, even though I found myself faced with the same overgrown wilderness which had greeted me when I landed in 1952.

This time, however, I had better tools, better stores, and in a way a much better start. For though the garden looked an overgrown tangle of vines and weeds, at least the ravening pigs had been eliminated so that the old banana trees were flourishing and my pawpaw shoots had grown up into sizable trees.

The fowls I had brought with me were thoroughly domesticated and this seemed to revive memories amongst the survivors of the flock I had abandoned six years before; so much so that almost as soon as they sighted me they came running for food. And even surveying what was left of their old run, I knew that, equipped with two 50-yard rolls of wire netting, the job of rebuilding it would be comparatively simple.

During those first weeks, I gradually tried to put the house in order. After I had mended the roof, I painted the inside of the kai room white, renovated the cookhouse and built a new and more permanent stove with an oven in which I could cook dishes from the more exciting ingredients I had brought with me. Since I now had milk powder, I was able to make myself a baked custard as soon as the hens started laying and even scones and pastry while my flour lasted.

POSTCRIPT

I left Suvarov on December 27, 1963. A variety of circumstances contributed to my decision.

The predominant reason was a very simple one. I realized I was getting on, and the prospect of a lonely death did not particularly appeal to me. I wasn't being sentimental about it, but the time had come to wake up from an exquisite dream before it turned into a nightmare.

I might have lingered on the island for a few more years, but a party of 11 pearl divers descended on Suvarov—and, frankly, turned my heaven into hell. They were happy-go-lucky Manihiki natives, and I didn't dislike them, but their untidiness, noise, and close proximity were enough to dispel any wavering doubts I might have had. Then, when I heard that more natives might be coming to dive for a couple of months each year in the lagoon, I resolved to leave with the divers.

I did so—and I have not regretted the decision. I am back in

Raro now, and you know, having proved my point—that I *could* make a go of it on a desert island and be happy alone—storekeeping doesn't after all seem such a monotonous job as it did in the years before 1952.

I have a wealth of memories that no man can take away from me and which I have enjoyed recalling in these pages. I hope you have enjoyed them, too.

Epilogue

Despite the Postscript, Tom Neale returned to his atoll again, in 1966, when the pearl divers left Suvarov. As recently as November 1972, he was reported, at the age of 71, happy and in good health on the South Pacific island of his own.

7

THE CAVES

ORDEAL AT SAND CAVE

HARRY ROSKOLENKO

Floyd Collins, a loner and professional cave-hunter, discovered the now-famous Crystal Cave in Kentucky in 1917, hoping that it would rival the world-famous Mammoth Cave as a sight-seeing attraction. Crystal Cave, however, was too far off the main dirt roads of those days, and despite all the work that Floyd Collins and his family did to make it a show-cave, the tourists were not coming.

Floyd Collins decided to explore elsewhere and he discovered Sand Cave. He had three partners, Doyle, Estes and Cox—all spelunkers— and Sand Cave was on Doyle's property. Often they worked in teams as they burrowed and dynamited, crawling deeper and farther through the narrow caverns, but most often Floyd Collins went off alone, seeking inner glowing chambers and cave cathedrals. On January 30, 1925, Floyd Collins was off alone, deep within Sand Cave—and this is what happened.

Drops of icy water dripped endlessly off the cave roof, falling with sickening finality on the still body of a man who lay trapped 50 feet below the earth. Outside, the sun shone brightly, and living men worked frantically to burrow down to the victim, but inside Sand Cave, the only sounds were the ceaseless dripping of water and the wail of a cold wind soughing through black tunnels the sun had never lighted.

The day before, Floyd Collins had wormed his way through an 18-inch opening in one of the inky vaults of Sand Cave. He was seeking an inner cave, a huge, domed cathedral of rock he believed existed below the surface and would prove to be larger and more beautiful than Mammoth Cave, the popular tourist attraction near Cave City, Kentucky.

Collins moved through the narrow tunnel slowly and cautiously, for he was an experienced cave explorer who had spent most of his boyhood and adult life investigating the wonders beneath the earth. He carried dynamite, a crowbar and a lamp. As he squirmed through the coffinlike opening, he noted that suspended above him was an enormous boulder, held in place only by a small rock.

He emerged from the tunnel and saw it—the cave of his dreams! He had come out into a vast inner chamber, many feet below the earth, studded with immense glittering stalactites and stalagmites. The ceiling was lofty, the length and width generous beyond his fondest hopes. He knew that at last he had discovered a cave more imposing than Mammoth. Now he would be rich, along with his partners Doyle, Estes and Cox. For the opening could be enlarged, and this cave would become the eighth wonder of the world, an attraction that would bring tourists flocking. Perhaps they would call it Collins Cave, and schoolchildren would be taught the date of its discovery: January 30, 1925.

Full of excitement and anxious to tell his partners and relatives the good news, Collins began the return trip to the surface. Once again he wedged himself into the narrow opening, inching along on his knees and elbows. Then it happened.

His foot brushed against the small stone holding the giant boulder in place. With a derisive whisper of rock on rock, the entire boulder dropped a few inches and crushed down on Collins's left ankle, smashing him to the earth and pinning him there as securely as if he had been nailed.

He twisted about frantically, pulling his leg up, trying to twist his ankle free. The seven-ton boulder was immovable. Scraping moisture from the walls of his coffin, he tried to wet his leg so that it might become slippery and slide from under the terrible weight pressing it down. This too failed. He grabbed his left knee with both hands and tugged until he feared his ankle was coming apart. It was no use. He was caught, held captive by the deep earth he considered his home. He lay back panting, trying to keep calm, trying to swallow the fear that welled up in him like a loathsome beast determined to devour him.

All this had happened 24 hours ago, for his hunger told him the time of day or night outside his tomb. Inside, it was always night—an endless night of pain and lonely terror. A few hours ago he had tried to move the boulder off his leg with the crowbar, but he couldn't budge the jagged mass. To make matters worse, his twistings and turnings loosened up sand and small rocks so that his body and face were soon covered. Hysterically he brushed it away, for he was being choked to death by the damp, clammy sand. He tried to sleep, but water dripped onto his face with maddening regularity. He lay back, numbed by the pain in his left leg, his body chilled by the cold of the cave. He was hoping, thinking, waiting—help would be along soon. It would come. It had to come!

Then he heard a scraping noise. He heard friendly voices. Then he saw a light! Estes and Doyle were coming through to him—at last! He became frantic, yelling to them, begging them to hurry up. After many minutes he saw Estes's son, Jewell, then Doyle, then Estes. They gaped at him, speechless, then squeezed into the narrow tomb, trying to move the boulder off Floyd's leg. It was impossible to stir it. Excited, tense, hungry, yet filled with hope, Floyd begged them to get his brothers, to get equipment, to get food. They left their lamp, crawling out hurriedly to get assistance.

Floyd's excitement grew, for he saw himself free soon, once again the master of his legs and his body, a human earthworm who satisfied some primitive urge as he crawled and wriggled through unknown tunnels. He recalled that his father had said on one Christmas, when Floyd had forgotten to return in time for dinner, "It's his kind of a church, I guess. . . ." And now Floyd was praying in his church, for the pain in his leg was getting worse. He took the lamp, shoved it over to get a better look at his leg, but became afraid. He would rather not know how badly he was hurt. All he knew was that his body was on a rack, but that he would soon be rescued. He lay back to wait.

Two hours later there was pandemonium as many farmers gathered at the entrance of the cave, spurred on by Floyd's brothers, Marshall and Homer. Homer crawled in with food and a rubber raincoat to keep the dripping water off Floyd's face. For eight hours Homer kept wiggling in and out, carrying away stone and sand in small bags, trying to widen the aperture, pausing on every trip to cheer up Floyd. Others crawled in with crowbars, but the boulder remained where it was, pinned on Floyd's left leg, a mass of stone squeezing his life away.

Homer, now almost hysterical about his brother's plight, offered $500 to any man who would rescue Floyd. Rumors began to circulate that Floyd was dying. Hooper, a local electrician, made the next attempt, but succeeded only in getting hot coffee through to Floyd, now in desperate condition after 48 hours of entombment. The entire congregation of the local church, led by the minister, volunteered to help. By the time the third day passed, many would-be rescuers had come and gone, some for the $500, others for humane reasons.

Cave City, meanwhile, had become an important place for photographers and reporters as news flashed around the world of Floyd's entombment. With the journalists came hordes of riffraff, bringing their local moonshine, to stage orgies and riots at the entrance of the cave. A newspaperman, in writing about the scene, described it adequately when he called the goings-on "Moonshine, Muck and Madness."

While the country hoodlums congregated on the outside, staging their drunken revels, inside, Floyd was becoming incoherent. More than 100 hours had passed, and he was still a prisoner under the boulder. The water now dripped on the raincoat, but its beat was drumming away his sanity; the freezing dampness of the cave was stiffening his body. He was reduced to the state of an infant, forced to urinate and defecate in his dungarees. Every volunteer now reported a collapse in Floyd's mental and physical condition. To Floyd these visitors were apparitions, ghostly figures of another world. He saw them in a daze as they squirmed close to him, struggling to free him. Outside, more than 15,000 people were surging about, clogging every byway leading to Sand Cave, making a carnival of the heroic attempts going on to save a human being from a living entombment.

Powerful air compressors and drills had been brought in, offered freely by engineering firms throughout the country. The drama, however, was turning into a bizarre tragicomedy, with the antics of the drunkards and the louts crowding about, keeping the rescuers from doing their best. When several monument builders arrived to survey the possibilities of a shaft being sunk, they were not allowed to get to the entrance of the cave by the mobs of drunkards and rioters. The rioting got so bad that Governor Fields called out the Kentucky State Militia to put an end to the orgy that reigned for several days. It was a sideshow to the tragedy still unfolding.

Lieutenant Robert A. Burdon, of the Louisville Fire Department, made the next rescue attempt, having designed a pulling harness which he put around Floyd's waist and shoulders. Floyd was but half-conscious now. The harness, however, almost tore Floyd apart without moving his leg one inch from beneath the boulder. W. B. Miller, of the *Louisville Courier,* then tried to lift the boulder with a jack, but the earth gave way, leaving the boulder still on Floyd's leg. Each rescuer, ironically, was loosening up the sides and the ceiling in his efforts, and their combined efforts, tragically, was to bring down tons of earth, eventually sealing off the aperture and the entrance.

Homer Collins, who had been hospitalized for intense fatigue, offered an additional $500 to any doctor willing to amputate Floyd Collins's left leg, and thus free him. But not a doctor stepped up. It would have been impossible, in any event, to carry on surgery in the narrow confines of the low-roofed tunnel, with the jagged stalactites threatening every movement.

Until the arrival of Henry St. George Tucker Carmichael, the general manager of the Kentucky Rock Asphalt Company, it was still amateur night at Sand Cave. Carmichael wheezed up in an old car with a plan to rescue Floyd. He would brace the opening and sink a connecting shaft from above. An hour before a volunteer had reported bad news—Collins was raving. He was feverish, staring from his prone position at the knifelike stalactites directly above his head. At 38, his stocky, dogged body, used to privations, was reaching the limits of human endurance. He was babbling like a child in a strange surrounding, unable to comprehend the walls of his cave-prison. He was losing his sanity under the tattoo of the dripping water, returning to dreams of childhood when everything was warm, clean and gentle.

With no time to lose, Carmichael, furnished with a tremendous array of mining equipment, set his crews to work. The shaft would go down 65 feet, then verge sideways and meet the chamber where Floyd lay entombed.

Volunteers trying to brace the entrance to the cave now reported a "tight squeeze"; *the floor and the ceiling were fusing!* Suddenly 15 feet of ceiling dropped between the entrance and where Floyd lay, encasing him beyond the cave-in, adding horror upon horror. Men dug desperately, removing tons of stone and sand, trying to keep open the line of communication to the trapped man. Outside, the mounds of excavated earth piled up, looking like a primitive burial ground.

Carmichael worked furiously to sink the shaft. It was "dig, dump and pray," he said, when they reached 45 feet after two days of digging. But at that depth the earth became treacherous. Avalanches began filling up the shaft as quickly as the miners dug it out. With but 20 feet to go, Carmichael decided to push through a lateral shaft and bypass the treacherous strata. But now, as if nature were conspiring against the rescue, a hard rain started, softening the earth and causing more cave-ins. A big canvas umbrella was rigged over the shaft to keep the rain out, but the shaft was sagging dangerously.

For Carmichael and his crews, it was a terrible ordeal. They were in a race against time, for Floyd had not been seen since the cave-in blocking the entrance and the narrow aperture. On Monday, February 16, after 11 days of fantastic labors, a miner named Brenner finally broke through. Brenner reported seeing the victim looking like a mummy in a tomb. The fingers of his left hand were stuck in his mouth. Floyd Collins was dead.

Carmichael went down to investigate and returned with the sad proof. It was all over now. Furthermore, the lateral shaft that had penetrated Floyd's tomb was in a critical condition, making it impossible to bring out the body. Two physicians stated that death had occurred two to four days before; that Floyd Collins, after 12 days of incarceration, had died of exposure and exhaustion.

There were many brave men at Sand Cave, with Carmichael heading the long list, followed by the cub reporter for the *Louisville Courier-Journal*, William Burke Miller, who won the Pulitzer Prize that year for his story of Floyd Collins. Not only was his reporting extraordinary, but he helped to operate the jack with Lieutenant Burdon.

On February 17 the cave was sealed and a burial service was read. Today the cave is an eternal mausoleum, dedicated to man's endless courage, to the great community of brave men who had participated in the ordeal and to Floyd Collins, the intrepid adventurer and discoverer of subterranean worlds. His father, Lee Collins, said at the service: "It is a fitting place, just like a church, for every cave was a church to Floyd. If he were here to tell us, he would say, 'I am content.' "

Epilogue

Several years later the cave was reopened and the body was removed. It now rests at the nearby Floyd Collins Crystal Cave, which has, at last, become a major attraction.

In 1954, a 60-man team that included cartographers, hydrologists, surveyors, meteorologists, photographers, doctors, nurses, cave scientists spent a week within the deepest, most difficult-to-crawl-through recesses of Crystal Cave, to plumb for Floyd Collins's never-told discoveries of 1917. Some areas of the long crawlways afforded but a ten-inch-high squeeze, difficult and dangerous for the most professional spelunker. But they discovered what Floyd Collins had found in 1917—an amazing series of underground cathedrals—as well as some empty food cans that Collins had left behind 37 years earlier.

The scientific expedition, organized by the National Speleological Society, mapped and photographed every area of Crystal Cave, taking away various geological samples. But one man, Floyd Collins, who went off with a lamp, a pick and dynamite, the solo caveman—who wrote his own epitaph at Sand Cave—was its discoverer.

8

THE MOUNTAINS

ADVENTURE—THE UNENDING CHALLENGE

Maurice Herzog

Writer, mountain climber, minister of sports under de Gaulle, Maurice Herzog is best known as the leader of the French mountain-climbing expedition that reached the austere Himalayan peak, Annapurna, 26,496 feet high, in 1950. He and his companion, Louis Lachenal, endured frostbite, snow blindness and on the way down from Annapurna, lost their way. They were the first to conquer an 8000-meter mountain—but Herzog lost all his toes and fingers before he came down from that mountain.

We live in an era of exploration—the British scaling Earth's "Third Pole," Everest; the Germans topping Nanga-Parbat; the Americans' gallant, tragic try for K-2; other expeditions, Japanese, Indian, Swiss, Norwegian, pursuing their goals on the roof of the world. Men have sounded great depths as well—Professor Piccard, Jacques-Yves Cousteau and others plumbing the eerie ocean bottoms, and the speleologists, the cave-plungers, groping farther and farther down into underground darkness. Why is all this going on? What makes men behave this way?

The answer is, the spirit of adventure—a yearning for the unknown, for risks, that moves Western men who live in modern "comfort," the heaven and hell of our days.

My own awakening to the magical spirit of adventure came in my university days. In Paris, I was a student, dividing my time between law and speculation in the pure sciences. Then, one February, I had the chance to go to the Alps. I came to a village peacefully hibernating among snow-covered mountains. I started at sunrise and climbed the lower mountain slopes until I came to a small forest. Far from any inhabited place, I had only myself to count on. The solitude suddenly made me feel extremely vulnerable. I had the sensation that my life was in danger. I was venturing alone up immense snow slopes. Avalanches were a constant threat.

I was part of nature, like an animal among other animals—white hares, marmots, chamois, jackdaws, foxes. I felt my muscles acting as muscles naturally should. I was steeped in brilliant sunshine, although I fought against the piercing cold. Finally, worn and hungry, I reached the crest. I had striven against nature like a primitive man to gain that goal, and suddenly I experienced a vast exultancy.

I believe that what I felt that day closely resembles what we call happiness. I also believe that if I felt such happiness in such rigorous circumstances it is because the planned, organized, predigested happiness that the modern world offers is not complete. It leaves certain sides of man's nature unsatisfied.

After all, man is only an animal with a big brain. He makes such a fuss about the brain that he forgets arms, legs, pectoral muscles, as if he were ashamed of them. A human being is constructed to defend his life—and not merely by trickery, malice or cunning. If we are here today it is because our ancestors learned how to fight against the elements and against other animals. If they could win those fights it was not only because they were crafty but also because they knew how to run, jump, strike, swim and climb; because they had a powerful physical mechanism, great vigor, incredible resistance and a skill and suppleness not combined in any other animal in creation.

Nowadays "comfort" means that the whole marvelous, miraculous organization of man's muscles may eventually become useless to him. Now he is still able to recapture the great primeval satisfaction of his forebears. He can be totally exhilarated. And this, indeed, is a sign that he is on the right road, that he is, at last, completely at one with himself.

All this has not gone unnoticed among the races which have managed to acquire the peak of worldly comfort. As life has grown progressively easier over the centuries, with adventure disappearing from the face of the earth, man's physical organism has protested. Society's solution is sport. It is notable that sports have developed most brilliantly in advanced societies. Sport has no meaning when daily life provides its parallel.

For the ultimate stage of our comfort-keyed civilization man will doubtless sustain himself by consuming a variety of little pills. But, just as swallowing nourishment through pills will never entirely supplant gourmandizing and the pleasures of the table, so sport will never abolish a thirst for natural activity without training manuals or tricks. And the solution is not a super-sport. The solution is adventure—adventure in which a man's total energies, all his physical and mental resources, are involved. In adventure, muscles, nerves, instincts, reflexes, even brains—in a word, the entire man—are taxed to the full.

Please understand me: everything that involves danger is not necessarily adventure. Often it is mere prowess, a gratuitous, barren exploit. Valid adventure, so far as I am concerned, is not pursued at all costs, or artificially created. A great French philosopher, Alain, recently dead, put it this way: "He who seeks adventure is condemned never to find it."

When a mountaineer decides to climb he foresees everything possible to foresee, organizes the smallest details of his ascent precisely so as to avoid "adventure." Those who do not proceed thus are mental cases who need a psychoanalyst and generally won't live long. Most mountaineers are anxious not to die. We are truly afraid of dangers and try from the start to be forewarned and to avoid them. Despite the general impression, we do not start off seeking adventure.

Often enough during a climb, however, circumstances arise

that put us in a difficult spot. Sometimes it is a rock or ice fall that we must avoid, sometimes a blizzard that threatens to overwhelm us; or it may be a track that leads us astray and cannot be retraced, a misplotting of our course bringing us to unscalable barriers, an injured comrade who must be carried back, the fall of darkness paralyzing an advance, a slip into a crevasse, fog in a wide snowfield confusing us into going in circles—a thousand such incidents, often several of them at once in a single day.

Face to face with these life-and-death crises, a man's real character appears. He is brave or cowardly, skillful or clumsy, patient or impulsive. Death stalks him and he must utilize all his forces to survive. All his qualities as a man are involved, and they must be complete. The slightest faltering, the slightest weakness, can be fatal.

No mountaineer exults in a ticklish situation. But when, thanks to energy and skill, he overcomes a critical obstacle or conquers an unforeseen emergency, he reacts with a kind of pride that seems to me legitimate. He has managed, unaided, to dominate hostile nature and he feels a great self-satisfaction —just as his ancestors must have felt when they had warded off the attack of a ferocious beast or slain a creature larger than themselves.

The true joy of living, simple as it may seem, is harder to manufacture than a jet engine. It must be in one's self—and then one must win it. The true value of life is never apparent until one has risked losing it. A man who has triumphed over mortal danger is born again. It is a birth without indebtedness to anything on earth. It endows one with a serenity and independence which are truly unutterable.

Mountain climbers, polar explorers, pioneers in unknown, hostile regions, in the caves of the earth and the sea's depths, are all linked by the same vision. All of them stake their native, human gifts against the unknown. Their reward is to enrich mankind's heritage, and the sense of this is their common bond.

When all the mountains in the world have been scaled, when the poles hold no more secrets, when the last acre of the last continent has been traversed, when, in short, everything on our planet is known and catalogued, the way will still be open for discovery. The world will never be conquered so long as the zest for conquest, for adventure, is in men's hearts.

THE ULYSSES FACTOR

J.R.L. ANDERSON

J.R.L. Anderson is an English writer-yachtsman, the author of *East of Suez, Vinland Voyage, The Greatest Race in the World,* and *The Ulysses Factor.*

It comes to most of us to be brought up wondering sharply, "What on earth am I doing here, anyway?" This question struck me with force in the cockpit of a small boat in the Davis Strait between Greenland and Labrador. It was a horrible night, with low clouds seeming to meet the sea and a wind that whipped spray from the wave tops to fling it stinging in your face. We worked single watches on that trip, and I was alone at the wheel, my five mates sleeping, or trying to sleep, below. I had an hour or so of my watch to go, and my hands were brutally cold. What on earth was I doing there and why?

I was there by my own volition, my own act, but could I help it? Of course I could help it, I need not have been there at all. My mates were there because I had asked them to come, but equally their response had been voluntary. So. One can help getting married, or joining the Army. But is either an entirely voluntary act? Man is an animal species, belonging to his particular herd: unless enough men marry, and at times of need

become soldiers, the herd dies. Was this relevant to my being
in a small sailing boat in the Davis Strait attempting to rediscover America, or at least to casting some light on how America
was discovered by the Norseman Leif Eriksson roughly a thousand years before we sailed? I thought perhaps it was relevant.

Since the ending of the Second World War in 1945, the world
has been much entertained, and a little excited, by the exploits
of individuals in undertaking self-imposed tasks that require
coming to terms in rather special ways with the elemental
forces of nature. Thor Heyerdahl and five companions crossed
the Pacific in or on a raft of balsa-wood. Edmund Hillary and the
Sherpa Tensing climbed Everest. Men did not exactly begin to
cross oceans in small boats, but did begin to do so rather frequently, and in very small craft. In 1951 Stanley Smith and
Charles Violet sailed the Atlantic by the stiff northern route in
the 20-foot yawl *Nova Espero*. Between November 1951 and
February 1952 Patrick Ellam and Colin Mudie crossed from
Casablanca to Barbados in *Sopranino*, an even smaller boat. In
May 1952 Ann Davison left Plymouth singlehanded in the 23-
foot sloop *Felicity Ann* and after calling at various ports in
France, Spain and North Africa reached Dominica on the other
side of the Atlantic in January 1953. In 1960 H.G. Hasler and
Francis Chichester laconically challenged one another to a *race*
across the Atlantic, and the Singlehanded Transatlantic Race
was born.

In these same decades less dramatically publicized people
undertook many exploits requiring at least equal determination
and endurance. That great mountaineer H.W. Tilman, who,
after climbing Nanda Devi with N.E. Odell, for a time held,
with Odell, the distinction of having reached the highest summit yet attained by man, decided to go to sea. At an age when
most men think of retirement, he sailed an old Bristol Channel
pilot cutter, *Mischief*, to Patagonia. Husband and wife teams,
the Hiscocks, the Pyes, the Smeetons adventured in small boats
in some of the most inhospitable seas in the world. Why?

I began to think rather deeply about this when I was myself in a fairly inhospitable sea in 1966. Since then the exploits have increased both in number and intensity. John Ridgway and Chay Blyth *rowed* an open dory across the Atlantic. Chichester *raced* himself, or the ghosts of the masters of the old clipper ships, singlehanded round the world. Alec Rose took a twenty-year-old boat singlehanded round the world. Robin Knox-Johnston sailed singlehanded round the world without putting into port or taking on supplies. Sheila Scott flew a single-engined light aeroplane round the world. Men, and a few, a very few, women continue such undertakings. Why?

Love of adventure, money (sometimes), desire for fame—the obvious and easy explanations seem to me not enough. They add words to things without explaining them—it is like "explaining" that a man has a pain in his hip because he has sciatica, which does nothing to indicate why he has sciatica, nor what it is. Human exploits accepting physical challenge *because* of the challenge have increased in number in recent decades, but in terms of the world's population the individuals who undertake them form a percentage so minute that it could reasonably be ignored as having any kind of significance. Yet trace elements in animal and plant growth, in proportions so tiny that sometimes their existence can only be inferred, are now known to be of vital importance to survival. Is there here a genetic factor of importance to human development, or even survival?

There are two forms of adaptation in the evolutionary process to which man, with all other living things, is subject. They are known as *general adaptation* and *special adaptation*. General adaptation is the ability of a species to acquire characteristics that assist survival over the whole range of conditions in which it lives—in man, for instance, the ability to communicate by speech, to make tools, to be more or less omniverous. Special adaptation is defined by Professor Carleton S. Coon in *The Origin of Races* as involving "the acquisition of a new trait, or trait complex, that is useful in a single environment, under special circumstances." He adds:

It is the process which enables an animal to resist heat, cold, or bright light, to see well in dim light, to run faster or swim better than its fellows, or to live without water in deserts. . . .

Men do extraordinary things in the hope of gain: a love of adventure coupled with a desire to make money may be explanation enough for all these feats of human endeavor. To write this is at once to dismiss it, for it is patently untrue. Men have beggared themselves, and done so coldly and deliberately, to build boats to cross an ocean for no apparent purpose, or to finance an expedition in search of no tangible treasure. Sometimes they have come across treasure, and have been glad enough, no doubt, to find it, but treasure-seeking in the ordinary sense cannot be the driving force I mean. Nor can that almost equally powerful motive, the lure of fame. Men like to be famous, and publicity of one sort or another has often been sought in connection with some enterprising feat. But sometimes the proposed feat is in itself an effort to attract notice to some project or manufacture, in which case it comes under quite another heading. Sometimes, particulary in recent years, publicity has been a method of trying to finance an expedition, but that does not make it necessarily the object of it. Sometimes a man dominated by the need to climb his mountain or to cross his unknown sea may have a considerable distaste for publicity at all. Of course, in some circumstances to shun publicity or to play hard-to-get is a method of courting notoriety, but certainly not always. Tilman, for example, any one of whose exploits could have made the name of a lesser man into a household word, has been content to be known to those who care to read his books. Adrian Hayter, whose remarkable first voyage in *Sheila* has never had the recognition it merited, is another who has sought no popular reputation for himself.

Neither gold nor fame will do. They may be won by a successful endeavor, but they do not explain this particular kind of endeavor. The anthropological approach remains: there is some factor in man, some form of special adaptation, which prompts a few individuals to exploits which, however purposeless they may seem, are of value to the survival of the race. I call this the Ulysses factor. But, if so, why is it manifest now; how, when the terrestrial globe is mapped and explored, its resources known, can there be any survival-value in crossing an ocean by the primitive means of sail or oars? . . .

A genetic factor exists potentially in all members of a given race, but its manifestations are Protean, it may be dormant over long periods, and its emergence in individuals may be idiosyncratic. Changes in environment may repress it, or intensify it. The Ulysses factor has been exceptionally manifest in different peoples at different times in history, profoundly influencing history. It is discernible in the Phoenicians around the tenth century B.C., in the Greeks about the eighth century B.C., in the Persians of the sixth century B.C., the Arabs of about the same time, or perhaps earlier. In more recent history the factor was a powerful driving force in the Scandinavian peoples of the eighth to the eleventh centures A.D., in the Portuguese and Spaniards of the fourteenth and fifteenth centuries, the British of the sixteenth century, the Dutch of the seventeenth, the British again and the French in the eighteenth century. At all these periods there were direct personal and national gains to be looked for in exploration, and it is impossible to disentangle the exploring factor in *man* from the commercial motives of the *men* who sought to profit from it. But it is hard to believe that Eriksson, Vasco da Gama, Magellan, Drake, Davis, Cook, Bouganville and their peers were animated solely by commercial motives. They could not have been: and although they served many different interests, they shared certain human characteristics, which indicate a common driving force, deep seated in all of them.

In the nineteenth century the factor underwent some degree of mutation. It was less obviously necessary for national survival to extend physical horizons, but the compelling need to extend horizons still manifested itself in individuals. In a letter to

Monckton Milnes (Lord Houghton) in 1863, when preparing to adventure up the Lower Congo, Sir Richard Burton wrote:

Starting in a hollowed log of wood some thousand miles up a river, with an infinitesimal prospect of returning, I ask myself Why? And the only echo is, "damned fool—the devil drives."

The devil? Burton's devil here was clearly an irresistible manifestation in him of the Ulysses factor. Livingstone and other great missionaries turned the factor to the service of religion. The missionary element in the religions of the world is, itself, a manifestation of this deep need in man to explore. To say this is not to decry the religious motive: God may use the obscure functioning of some human gland as readily as the work of human hands. The Ulysses factor was strong in St. Paul—had it not been, the Christian Church might have been markedly different. It was strong in St. Francis Xavier, and has been so in many of his followers.

With the dwindling scope for physical exploration of the world, men invented new goals. Mountaineering for its own sake was a nineteenth-century invention. Travellers have always climbed mountains when they had to, but if there was a pass to the far side they took it thankfully. Edward Whymper looked to the great peaks of the Alps and felt that they had to be climbed because they were there. This ideal inspired first the English and very soon the French and the Italians: the Alpine Club was founded and mountaineering was born. After the Alps, men looked to the greater peaks of the Himalayas and the Andes. Few people can hope to make money out of climbing mountains: most mountaineers spend money in order to climb. Theirs is another manifestation of the Ulysses factor. Its philosophical implications I shall discuss later.

At the turn of the twentieth century the poles had still to be reached, and to get to them became in individuals an intense physical desire, stimulated by intense national rivalry. Peary (American) achieved the North Pole in 1909. Amundsen

(Norwegian) the South in 1911, beating Scott (British) by a few weeks. Shackleton (British) attempted to cross the Antarctic Continent in 1913: heroic failure put him with the immortals.

The war of 1914–1918 called on every faculty in man. In war there is manifold activity for the Ulysses factor, but it is confused in the herd instincts of fighting nations. . . .

After the war Everest remained as a kind of special challenge to human endeavor, inspiring attempt after attempt to climb it. Irvine and Mallory died on the mountain in 1924: whether either reached the summit is unknown. In 1936 Tilman and Odell climbed Nanda Devi (25,645 ft), then the highest mountain in the world to have been climbed. In 1950 Maurice Herzog and Louis Lachenal climbed Annapurna (26,492 ft). Other great peaks felt the foot of man, but Everest (29,028 ft) remained the final challenge (unless either Irvine or Mallory had won an unknown victory) until 1953, when Hillary and Tensing climbed it, in the expedition led by John Hunt (Lord Hunt).

Final challenge? No sooner was Everest climbed by one route than men began to study other, perhaps more difficult, ways of getting to the top. The Ulysses factor is Protean. Thoughts returned to the Alps, to the north face of the Eiger and other routes once considered impossible to summits already reached. And new challenges appeared at sea.

The Ulysses factor appears to be unique to man. Other animals have a sense of adventure and certainly enjoy hunting, but deliberate risk-taking in pursuit of a goal of no apparent practical value is not the habit of any animal other than man. In man the factor can be an urge as compelling as sex. Like sex, indeed with all other human attributes, the Ulysses factor can be exploited and abused; it can take a psychological wrong turning and become inimical to survival. That is one reason why it should be studied. Again like sex, manifestations of the factor in individuals may stimulate powerful mass excitement: the crowds assembled to greet Chichester or Rose tingle with a sort of static electrical excitement not dissimilar to that felt in a crowd gathered to see an exceptionally beautiful film-star. This is because the factor is present in mankind as such, and although it may be dormant in the great majority of individuals, it will respond unconsciously to some exploit that excites it.

Historically, the factor has appeared most strongly in communities either dominant or about to become dominant—in the Scandinavians at the peak of Viking expansion, in the British in the sixteenth to the nineteenth centuries. Up to this century there is a distinct relationship between the occurrence of the Ulysses factor in the people of a nation and that nation's position in the world: when the factor is strong in individuals it assists national dominance. But there seems to have been a mutation here. In the decades since the Second World War, when Britain's power as a nation has been declining, the factor has been more strongly apparent in the British than in any other national community. Other outstanding manifestations have been in the Norwegians and the French, neither now a great power in the old sense. But what is national greatness?

ERIC SHIPTON—THE MAN WHO FOUND HIMSELF

J.R.L. Anderson

Eric Shipton was the architect of man's victory over Everest. He did not climb the mountain, but without him it may be doubted if it would yet have been climbed. His was the inspiration behind the British expedition under Sir John Hunt (Lord Hunt) in 1953 which achieved the summit: his years of exploring in the high Himalaya provided the strategical planning for success; Tensing, the Sherpa who reached the top with Hillary, had been recruited by him. Shipton was originally selected by the Himalayan Committee to lead the 1953 expedition, and he had started work on it when he was replaced by Hunt. Why remains a mystery. Shipton himself, in his autobiography published in 1969, can say only:

The influences which caused the Committee's *volte face* are still obscure.*

It is well, perhaps, that they should remain so, for the incident is not a happy one in British mountaineering. But Ulysses was not an administrator. He was content to lead the way. So is Shipton. He is too full a man to be embittered by this piece of

*This and all other quotations from Eric Shipton in this chapter are from his autobiography *That Untravelled World*. Hodder & Stoughton, 1969.

curious treatment. His place in mountaineering history will grow with time.

Shipton found more than unmapped routes in mountains by obeying the Ulysses factor in him. He found himself. His whole life has been a manifestation of the factor. He was born in 1907 in Ceylon, where his father was a tea-planter. When he was two his father died, and he had a wandering early childhood, his mother travelling restlessly from place to place to Ceylon, India, England and France. In 1914 his mother remarried, but he boy scarcely knew his stepfather, as he was killed in action in 1917.

Shipton has all the far-ranging intelligence that is characteristic of the Ulysses factor, but it did not emerge at school. His childhood had been too unsettled for him to adapt readily to a conventional English preparatory school. He was supposed to go on to Harrow, but failed to pass Common Entrance. He read Whymper's books on mountains, and when he went with a schoolfriend for a walking tour in Norway he found absolute contentment. He writes of his boyhood experience:

As yet my ambitions were not focused on any one aspect of travel, and I would have been equally enchanted by a desert, a polar ice-cap or a tropical forest. I was very intrigued by volcanic phenomena and had collected a number of books on the subject; the only classical writing which stirred my interest was Pliny's account of the eruption of Vesuvius, and that, naturally, in an English translation and not in the course of my Latin studies. . . . I acquired books by some of the early Alpine mountaineers and was thrilled to read in these the expression of so much of my own inarticulate feelings. . . . It was Whymper with his simple approach and exciting narrative, his lively observation and power of description, who most captivated me.

When he was 21 Shipton went to Kenya with the intention of becoming a farmer. By then he had served his apprenticeship to climbing in the Alps, and in time off from farming he made for the ten little-explored highlands of East and Central Africa.

With the distinguished Cambridge Mountaineer Wyn Harris, then in the Colonial Service in Kenya, he made the first ascent of Nelion, one of the twin peaks of Mount Kenya. In 1930, after an account of one of his climbs had appeared in the *East African Standard*, he got a letter from another Kenya planter asking for advice on climbing in East Africa. His name was H.W. Tilman. Shipton and Tilman made a number of African climbs together. That was the beginning of a trail of adventure that took both men to Everest and to the exploration of mountain ranges in the farthest parts ot the earth.

Tilman was nearly 33 to Shipton's 23 when they met, but at that time Shipton was the more experienced climber. Each man learned much from the other. They are curiously alike, and sharply dissimilar. Both have the Ulysses factor in them to a high degree, both have been moved by it throughout their lives. Neither can be content with a known horizon: to each a horizon, any horizon, beckons irresistibly—it is a screen of mist that *must* be penetrated, a curtain that *must* be drawn back. Both are magnificent climbers, and both climb to get *beyond* their mountains, not merely to get to the top. They are mountain-explorers rather than mountaineers, pleased with a first ascent if it comes their way, but not particularly competitive in their climbing. If Shipton had been more competitive he would no doubt have led the expedition that finally climbed Everest. He would also have been less interesting as a man.

Both Shipton and Tilman manifest the Ulysses factor in exceptional purity of form, but they are different forms. Shipton's compulsion to explore is fundamentally to discover himself; Tilman's is an external curiosity. Tilman is self-sufficient to the point of austerity. Shipton is self-sufficient in action, ready to be responsible for himself, but for him experience is not complete unless he can share it. Writing of his mother, he makes a revealing observation about himself.

I was very fond of my mother; but though we had a great deal in common we were never very close. This was largely due to her reticence which prevented intimate discussion, an indulgence to which I have always been addicted.

Shipton's eccentric childhood exaggerated tendencies already in him. Impatience with formal schooling is characteristic of the Ulysses factor: he had this impatience, which, added to the inability of a conventional prep-school to understand him, led him to assume that he was no good at learning and incapable of passing examinations. The intellectual power of his later work makes nonsense of both assumptions, but they were facts of his adolescence and intensified his passion for taking to the hills—here was something he *was* good at, a way of life with which he could come to terms.

In 1931, when he was 24, Shipton had to decide between two opportunities. Some friends of his in Kenya discovered alluvial gold and offered him a partnership in working it; and he was invited to join an expedition to attempt to climb Kamet (25,447 feet) in the Himalaya. He chose Kamet. The expedition, led by Frank Smythe, was successful, achieving what was then the first summit over 25,000 feet to be climbed. In the following year Shipton was invited to join an expedition to Everest led by Hugh Ruttledge. That was the Everest expedition of 1933, which succeeded in establishing a camp at 27,400 feet, but could not reach the summit.

Shipton was now becoming recognized as among the ablest of Himalayan climbers. With Tilman in 1934 he made a remarkable journey to survey the approaches to Nanda Devi, laying the groundwork for Tilman's great ascent of Nanda Devi in 1936. Shipton did not share that climb in 1936 because he was taking part in yet another Everest expedition. From then until the war he travelled extensively in the Himalaya and Karakoram ranges, filling in a number of blank spaces on the map and adding much to geographical knowledge. He travelled light, and kept himself by writing and lecturing on his visits to England.

He was on Everest again in 1938, and in 1939 returned to the

Karakoram for another great exploring journey in this wild part
of the roof of the world in Central Asia. That journey was interrupted by the war.

Again Shipton had a choice of paths. He was in remote country with a surveying tasks of obvious value to be done. War had
been declared for a month when his party first picked up news
of it by radio. Should he carry on as if nothing had happend?
There was precedent for this. Shackleton was on his way to the
Antarctic when war was declared in 1914: he had held it to be
his job to carry on.

Hard as it was to leave his mountains, Shipton went back to
India and offered his services to the (then British) Government
of India in any capacity that might seem useful. His two companions managed to get back to England. Shipton joined the
Indian Army.

His unique knowledge of Central Asia was soon needed. In
1940 he was sent as British Consul-General to Kashgar in Sinkiang. It was an important post. Sinkiang, north of Tibet, was,
nominally, subject to China, but for decades it had been run by
local war-lords and Russian influence was strong. The Consul-
General was the sole British representative in this strategically
important part of Central Asia. Shipton stayed for two years,
and did a remarkable job in a weird political setting. He was
relieved in 1942 and after doing various other war-time jobs he
was sent back to Kashfar in 1946. He stayed there for another
two years and then went as Consul-General to Kunming, in
Yunnan in Southern China. This was a time of great difficulty
as the Communist revolution spread throughout China. In due
course Kunming was taken over, the British Consulate-General
was closed and Shipton had to go. Two weeks after he got back
to England in 1951 he was invited to lead another expedition
to Everest.

Pre-war attempts to climb Everest had been made through
Tibet. The Chinese occupation of Tibet after the war made this
impracticable, so a new approach to the mountain was sought

from Nepal. This southern, or rather, southwestern route was the one by which Everest was climbed in 1953. It was Shipton's reconnaissance in 1951 that found the way. His removal from the leadership of the triumphant expedition of 1953 was a wry acknowledgment of his immense contribution to Himalayan climbing.

Shipton refused to be embittered by this shock; but inevitably it was a severe one, both emotionally and in its practical effect on his affairs. He had given up everything else to lead the Everest expedition, and now he had no job. He could have hoped for another consular post, but there was nothing immediately available. Finally, he got a job as warden of an Outward Bound school. Then his marriage broke up.

Ulysses shipwrecked does not sit on the beach and wring his hands. Shipton's whole life was shipwrecked and he reacted in characteristic fashion. He went to the hills on the Welsh border and found himself a job as a forestry laborer. He was close on 50.

Shipton the woodcutter might be content to forget the world, but the world was less ready to forget Shipton the explorer. In 1957—the year he reached 50—he was invited by the Imperial College of Science to return to the Karakoram with a party of students. He did, and although he went back to casual laboring after the Karakoram trip, "the enchantment of that untravelled world [as he puts it] had once more cast its compulsive spell." The greatest explorer of his generation in Central Asia turned to a wholly new field in the still more remote ranges of the Southern Andes.

The main outlines of Patagonia and Tierra del Fuego have long been known, but the interior, guarded by a formidable coast and the great Patagonian ice-cap, remained largely unexplored before Shipton's first Patagonian journey in 1958–1959. By that journey, and three subsequent expeditions in 1959–60, 1960–1961 and 1961–1962, Shipton mapped an unknown world. He also helped to settle peacefully a boundary dispute between Argentina and Chile. In his sixtieth year he went to have a look at the mountains of Alaska.

> I cannot rest from travel: I will drink Life to the lees. . . .

Shipton has had one objective throughout his life—to find out. His journeys have had secondary purposes: to collect botanical specimens, to study the behavior of glaciers, to climb a particular mountain, many such things. But always the real driving force in him has been to climb the ridge to see beyond it. He has added materially to human knowledge in many fields; more importantly, by discovering himself through his own exploring instinct he has inspired, and will continue to inspire, others to self-fulfillment.

His adventures had needed scale, the immense distances of Central Asia and the Andes. As the scope for acquiring wholly new geographical knowledge contracts—as Shipton has himself helped to contract it—can the scale on which the Ulysses impulse may be satisfied diminish? Can the mastery of mountaineering techniques satisfy the exploring instinct of the mountaineer? It could not satisfy Shipton. He has written of himself:

> For a while I was fascinated by the sheer technique of moving safely and easily over difficult ground; but even then I regarded the art as a means to an end, and neither reached nor aspired to more than a modest standard of climbing proficiency. After Mount Kenya I became less and less concerned with the mastery of technical difficulty, or even the ascent of individual peaks, but more and more absorbed in the problems and delights of movement over wide areas of mountain country. It was not that I lost any of my enjoyment in climbing peaks but simply that I found the other more rewarding.

Since the war much mountaineering effort has gone into the devising of techniques for climbing difficult rock-faces, often requiring the use of equipment that makes a climb in some sense artificial. But is a horizon less a horizon because it is only inches away? If those inches are a gap demanding every faculty of human courage and ingenuity to cross, the attainment of the far side may bring satisfaction not less real because its scale is small. To find a way to scale a wall of rock hitherto held to be unclimbable may be a discovery as rewarding as finding an unknown mountain. There is a slight but interesting mutation in the factor here. Shipton has needed mountain ranges, but the Ulysses factor may also manifest itself by sending men to single rock-faces. These two types of manifestations now exist side by side: there are men who climb in order to go somewhere else, and men who climb to get to the top. Shipton is an example of the former, but he respects both. The two British attempts to climb Annapurna in 1970 by routes deliberately selected for their technical difficulty are examples of the latter. Shipton sums up:

Personally, I welcome wholeheartedly the advance of modern techniques because it has widened the bounds of mountain adventure. There was a time, long ago, when I was oppressed by the thought that soon there would be no new peaks to climb and no new routes to explore. But the more I travelled in the remoter ranges of the world —Karakoram, Kuen Lun, Alaska, Southern Andes—the more I realised how vast is the field of fresh endeavour even for the traditional mountaineer. With the application of these new climbing and survival techniques the horizon is truly boundless.

Shipton has always manifested a true Ulysses caution in risk-taking. He has taken risks often enough in his adventurous life, but he has taken them only when he had to, and he has tried to calculate risks carefully. In his view a narrow escape from danger is not a matter for pride, but something to be ashamed of—the escape ought not to have been narrow. He considers the *motive* all-important in judging whether a risk is reasonable or not. If some risky course of action is followed out of foolhardiness, to try to win applause or simply to better someone else's performance, then it is to be condemned. If a risk has to be taken in the course of a journey it must be accepted as a reasonable hazard of life. Its possible consequences should be assessed, and the leader of the expedition taking it should be sure of his moral and physical resources for meeting them.

Shipton's clear-headed assessment of risks is well illustrated by his expedition to the Cordillera Darwin, an almost unexplored range of mountains running from Tierra del Fuego through the mass of rocky islands ending with Cape Horn. He was taken to the mouth of an unexplored inlet by a Chilean naval vessel, and here, with three companions and supplies for eight weeks, he cast off in a rubber dinghy. At the head of the unknown inlet the party was fortunate in finding a good rock route up a glacier, and the weather was kindly. Shipton left nothing to luck. He and his companions carried supplies for six weeks to a base camp above the forest line, and on all expeditions from their base camp they buried supplies at intervals against the return journey. Wherever they made a supply dump they took bearings with two compasses, checked against each other. It was as well, for on a ridge of Monte Darwin, the highest peak of the range, they were caught by a storm and a bag containing two days' food was lost. They took no gamble on improvement in the weather, but at once cut their daily ration by one-third. In fact, the weather did improve, and they were able to climb Monte Darwin and set off on the journey back to their base camp sooner than they thought. On the way back, however, the weather worsened and they met severe gales and heavy snow. Again they cut their rations, but did not worry much because of the food they had dumped on the outward journey. When they came to the site of their food dump, however, the whole area was under six feet of snow. Without their carefully checked compass bearings they could never have found the food: as it was it took them two hours of digging in the snow to locate the dump. But they did find it. Without ruthless self-discipline in taking precautions this incident of their journey might easily have become a tragedy.

The Ulysses impulse in Shipton led to the British conquest of Everest and enhanced the prestige of Britain at a time when the greatness of an imperial past seemed to be ebbing away. At a critical time of the war it ensured that a man with firsthand knowledge was available for a diplomatic post of the most delicate importance in Central Asia. Shipton the explorer has served his country well. Shipton the man found himself on the windswept ridges of his mountains to join that small company of individuals who have enriched humanity by living fully as themselves.

CRATERS OF FIRE

Haroun Tazieff

Geologist, speleologist, explorer, adventurer, scientist and photographer, Tazieff witnessed the eruption of Kituro in the Congo in 1948. We get the volcanic essence in his extraordinary description of the flaming flow at the edge of the crater of Kituro. The fiery power and splendor of nature's dynamite blowing its top is awesome in its seething and arresting spectacle.

THE CRATER OF KITURO

Standing on the summit of the growling cone, even before I got my breath back after the stiff climb, I peered down into the crater.

I was astonished. Two days previously the red lava had been boiling up to the level of the gigantic lip; now the funnel seemed to be empty. All that incandescent magma had disappeared, drawn back into the depths by the reflux of some mysterious ebb and flow, a sort of breathing. But there, about fifty feet below where I was standing, was the glow and the almost animate fury of the great throat which volcanologists call the conduit or chimney. It was quite a while before I could tear my

eyes away from that lurid fiery center, that weird palpitation of
the abyss. At intervals of about a minute, heralded each time by
a dry clacking, bursts of projectiles were flung up, running away
up into the air, spreading out fanwise, all aglare, and then falling back, whistling, on the outer sides of the cone. I was rather
tense, ready to leap aside at any moment, as I watched these
showers, with their menacing trajectories.

Each outburst of rage was followed by a short lull. Then heavy
rolls of brown and bluish fumes came puffing out, while a
muffled grumbling, rather like that of some monstrous watch-
dog, set the whole bulk of the volcano quivering. There was not
much chance for one's nerves to relax, so swiftly did each follow
on the other—the sudden tremor, the burst, the momentary
intensification of the incandescence, and the outbreak of a fresh
salvo. The bombs went roaring up, the cone of fire opening out
overhead, while I hung in suspense. Then came the hissing and
sizzling, increasing in speed and intensity, each "whoosh" ending up in a muffled thud as the bomb fell. On their black bed
of scoriae, the clots of molten magma lay with the fire slowly
dying out of them, one after the other growing dark and cold.

Some minutes of observation were all I needed. I noted that
today, apart from three narrow zones to the west, north, and
northeast, the edges of the crater had scarcely been damaged
at all by the barrage from underground. The southern point
where I stood was a mound rising some twelve or fifteen feet
above the general level of the rim, that narrow, crumbling lip
of scoriae nearer to the fire, where I had never risked setting
foot. I looked at this rather alarming ledge all round the crater,
and gradually felt an increasing desire to do something about
it. . . . It became irresistible. After all, as the level of the column
of lava had dropped to such an exceptional degree, was this not
the moment to try what I was so tempted to do and go right
round the crater?

Still, I hesitated. This great maw, these jaws sending out heat
that was like the heavy breathing of some living creature,

thoroughly frightened me. Leaning forward over that hideous glow, I was no longer a geologist in search of information, but a terrified savage.

"If I lose my grip," I said aloud, "I shall simply run for it."

The sound of my own voice restored me to normal awareness of myself. I got back my critical sense and began to think about what I could reasonably risk trying. "*De l'audace, encore de l'audace.* . . ." That was all very well, of course, but one must also be careful. Past experience whispered a warning not to rush into anything blindly. Getting the upper hand of both anxiety and impatience, I spent several minutes considering, with the greatest of care, the monster's manner of behaving. Solitude has got me into the habit of talking to myself, and so it was more or less aloud that I gave myself permission to go ahead.

"Right, then. It can be done."

I turned up my collar and buttoned my canvas jacket tight at the throat—I didn't want a sly cinder down the back of my neck! Then I tucked what was left of my hair under an old felt hat that did service for a helmet. And now for it!

Very cautiously indeed, I approach the few yards of pretty steep slope separating the peak from the rim I am going to explore. I cross, in a gingerly manner, a first incandescent crevasse. It is intense orange in color and quivering with heat, as though opening straight into a mass of glowing embers. The fraction of a second it takes me to cross it is just long enough for it to scorch the thick cord of my breeches. I get a strong whiff of burned wool.

A promising start, I must say!

Here comes a second break in the ground. Damn it, a wide one, too! I can't just stride across this one: I'll have to jump it. The incline makes me thoughtful. Standing there, I consider the unstable slope of scoriae that will have to serve me for a landing ground. If I don't manage to pull up . . . if I go rolling along down this funnel with the flames lurking at the bottom of

it . . . My little expedition all at once strikes me as thoroughly
rash, and I stay where I am, hesitating. But the heat under my
feet is becoming unbearable. I can't endure it except by shifting
around. It only needs ten seconds of standing still on this enemy
territory, with the burning gases slowly and steadily seeping
through it, and the soles of my feet are already baking hot.
From second to second the alternative becomes increasingly
urgent: I must jump for it or retreat.

Here I am! I have landed some way down the fissure. The
ashes slide underfoot, but I stop without too much trouble. As
so often happens, the anxiety caused by the obstacle made me
overestimate its importance.

Step by step, I set out on my way along the wide wall of
slaglike debris that forms a sort of fortification all round the
precipice. The explosions are still going on at regular intervals
of between sixty and eighty seconds. So far no projectile has
come down on this side, and this cheers me up considerably.
With marked satisfaction I note that it is pretty rare for two
bombs of the same salvo to fall less than three yards apart: the
average distance between them seems to be one of several
paces. This is encouraging. One of the great advantages of this
sort of bombardment, compared with one by artillery, lies in
the relative slowness with which the projectiles fall, the eye
being able to follow them quite easily. Furthermore, these
shells don't burst. But what an uproar, what an enormous, pro-
longed bellowing accompanies their being hurled out of the
bowels of the earth!

I make use of a brief respite in order to get quickly across the
ticklish northeastern sector. Then I stop for a few seconds, just
long enough to see yet another burst gush up and come shower-
ing down a little ahead of me, after which I start out for the
conquest of the northern sector. Here the crest narrows down
so much that it becomes a mere ridge, where walking is so
difficult and balancing so precarious that I find myself forced to
go on along the outer slope, very slightly lower down. Little by

little, as I advance through all this tumult, a feeling of enthusiasm is overtaking me. The immediate imperative necessity for
action has driven panic far into the background. And under the
hot, dry skin of my face, taut on forehead and cheekbones, I can
feel my compressed lips parting, of their own accord, in a smile
of sheer delight. But look out!

A sudden intensification of the light warns me that I am
approaching a point right in the prolongation of the fiery chimney. In fact, the chimney is not vertical, but slightly inclined in
a northwesterly direction, and from here one can look straight
down into it. These tellurian entrails, brilliantly yellow, seem to
be surging with heat. The sight is so utterly amazing that I stand
there, transfixed.

Suddenly, before I can make any move, the dazzling yellow
changes to white, and in the same instant I feel a muffled tremor
all through my body and there is a thunderous uproar in my
ears. The burst of incandescent blocks is already in full swing.
My throat tightens as, motionless, I follow with my gaze the
clusters of red lumps rising in slow, perfect curves. There is an
instant of uncertainty. And then down comes the hail of fire.

This time the warning was too short: I am right in the middle
of it all. With my shoulders hunched up, head drawn back, chin
in air, buttocks as much tucked in as possible, I peer up into the
vault of sinister whining and whizzing there above me. All
around bombs are crashing down, still pasty and soft, making a
succession of muffled *plops*. One dark mass seems to have sin-
gled me out and is making straight for my face. Instinctively I
take a leap to one side, and *feel* the great lump flatten itself out
a few inches from my left foot. I should like to have a look, but
this is not the moment! Here comes another projectile. I take
another leap to dodge it. It lands close beside me. Then suddenly the humming in the air begins to thin out. There are a
few more whizzing sounds, and then the downpour is over.

Have you ever tried to imagine a snail's state of mind as it
creeps out of its shell again, the anger past? That was the way

my head, which had been drawn back between hunched-up shoulders, gradually began to rise up again on my neck, and my arched back began to straighten, my arms to loosen, my hands to unclench. Right, then—it's better not to hang about in this sector! So I set out again. By this time I have got round three-quarters of the crater, and am in the gap between the northern and western zones, which are those that get the worst pounding. From here I can get back on the ridge proper.

I am now almost directly over the roaring chasm, and my gaze goes straight down into it like a stone dropping into the pit. After all, it's nothing but a tunnel. That's all. It's a vertical tunnel, ten or fifteen yards across, its walls heated to such a degree that they stretch and "rise" like dough, and up from its depths every now and then enormous drops of liquid fire spurt forth, a great splashing sweat that falls and vanishes, golden flash upon flash, back into the dazzling gulf. Even the brownish vapors emanating from the pit cannot quite veil its splendor. It is nothing but a tunnel running down into viscous cooper-colored draperies; yet it opens into the very substance of another world. The sight is so extraordinary that I forget the insecurity of my position and the hellish burning under the soles of my feet. Quite mechanically, I go on lifting first the left foot, then the right. It is as though my mind were held fast in a trap by the sight of this burning well from which a terrifying snore continually rises, interrupted by sharp explosions and the rolling of thunder.

Suddenly I hurl myself backward. The flight of projectiles has whizzed past my face. Hunched up again, instinctively trying to make as small a target of myself as I can, I once more go through the horrors that I am beginning to know. I am in the thick of this hair's-breadth game of anticipation and dodging.

And now it's all over; I take a last glance into the marvelous and terrible abyss, and am just getting ready to start off on the last stage of this burning circumnavigation, all two hundred yards of it, when I get a sudden sharp blow in the back. A delayed-action bomb! With all the breath knocked out of me, I stand rigid.

A moment passes. I wonder why I am not dead. But nothing seems to have happened to me—no pain, no change of any sort. Slowly I risk turning my head, and at my feet I see a sort of huge red loaf with the glow dying out of it.

I stretch my arms and wriggle my back. Nothing hurts. Everything seems to be in its proper place. Later on, examining my jacket, I discovered a brownish scorchmark with slightly charred edges, about the size of my hand, and I drew from it a conclusion of immense value to me in future explorations: so long as one is not straight in the line of fire, volcanic bombs, which fall in a still pasty state, but already covered with a kind of very thin elastic skin, graze one without having time to cause a deep burn.

I set off at a run, as lightly as my 165 pounds allow, for I must be as quick as I can in crossing this part of the crater edge, which is one of the most heavily bombarded. But I am assailed by an unexpected blast of suffocating fumes. My eyes close, full of smarting tears. I am caught in a cloud of gas forced down by the wind. I fight for breath. It feels as if I were swallowing lumps of dry, corrosive cotton wool. My head swims, but I urge myself at all costs to get the upper hand. The main thing is not to breathe this poisoned air. Groping, I fumble in a pocket. Damn, not this one. How about this other one, then? No. At last I get a handkerchief out and, still with my eyes shut, cover my mouth with it. Then, stumbling along, I try to get through the loathsome cloud. I no longer even bother to pay any attention to the series of bursts from the volcano, being too anxious to get out of this hell before I lose grip entirely. I am getting pretty exhausted, staggering. . . . The air filtered through the handkerchief just about keeps me going, but it is still too poisonous, and there is too little of it for the effort involved in making this agonizing journey across rough and dangerous terrain. The gases are too concentrated, and the great maw that is belching them forth is too near.

A few steps ahead of me I catch a glimpse of the steep wall of the peak, or promontory, from the other side of which I started about a century ago, it seems to me now. The noxious mists are licking round the peak, which is almost vertical and twice the height of a man. It's so near! But I realize at once that I shall never have the strength to clamber up it.

In less than a second, the few possible solutions to this life-and-death problem race through my mind. Shall I turn my back to the crater and rush away down the outer slope, which is bombarded by the thickest barrages? No. About face and back along the ledge? Whatever I do, I must turn back. And then make my escape. By sliding down the northern slope? This is also under too heavy bombardment. And the worst of it would be that in making a descent of that sort there would be no time to keep a watch for blocks of lava coming down on me.

Only one possibility is left: to make my way back all along the circular ridge, more than a hundred yards of it, till I reach the eastern rim, where neither gas nor projectiles are so concentrated as to be necessarily fatal.

I swing round. I stumble and collapse on all fours, uncovering my mouth for an instant. The gulp of gas that I swallow hurts my lungs, and leaves me gasping. Red-hot scoriae are embedded in the palms of my hands. I shall never get out of this!

The first fifteen or twenty steps of this journey back through the acrid fumes of sulphur and chlorine are a slow nightmare; no step means any progress and no breath brings any oxygen into the lungs. The threat of bombs no longer counts. Only these gases exist now. Air! Air!

I came to myself again on the eastern rim, gasping down the clean air borne by the wind, washing out my lungs with deep fresh gulps of it, as though I could never get enough. How wide and comfortable this ledge is! What a paradise compared with the suffocating, torrid hell from which I have at last escaped! And yet this is where I was so anxious and so tense less than a quarter of an hour ago.

Several draughts of the prevailing breeze have relieved my

agony. All at once, life is again worth living! I no longer feel that
desire to escape from here as swiftly as possible. On the contrary, I feel a new upsurge of explorer's curiosity. Once more
my gaze turns toward the mouth, out of which sporadic bursts
of grapeshot are still spurting forth. Now and then there are
bigger explosions and I have to keep a lookout for what may
come down on my head, which momentarily interrupts the
dance I keep up from one foot to the other, that *tresca* of which
Dante speaks—the dance of the damned, harried by fire. True,
I have come to the conclusion that the impact of these bombs
is not necessarily fatal, but I am in no hurry to verify the observation.

The inner walls of the crater do not all incline at the same
angle. To the north, west and south, they are practically vertical, not to say overhanging, but here on the east the slope drops
away at an angle of no more than fifty degrees. So long as one
moved along in a gingerly way, this might be an incline one
could negotiate. It would mean going down into the very heart
of the volcano. For an instant I am astounded by my own foolhardiness. Still, it's really too tempting. . . .

Cautiously, I take a step forward . . . then another . . . and
another . . . seems all right . . . it *is* all right. I begin the climb
down, digging my heels as deep as I can into the red-hot scoriae.
Gradually below me, the oval of the enormous maw comes
nearer, growing bigger, and the terrifying uproar becomes
more deafening. My eyes, open as wide as they will go, are
drunken with its monstrous glory. Here are those ponderous
draperies of molten gold and copper, so near—so near that I feel
as if I, human being that I am, had entered right into their
fabulous world. The air is stifling hot. I am right in the fiery
furnace.

I linger before this fascinating spectacle. But then, by sheer
effort, I tear myself away. It's time to get back to being "scientific" and measure the temperatures, of the ground, and of the
atmosphere. I plunge the long spike of the thermometer into

the shifting scoriae, and the steel of it glitters among these brownish and gray screes with their dull shimmer. At a depth of six inches the temperature is two hundred and twenty degrees centigrade. It's amusing to think that when I used to dream it was always about polar exploration!

Suddenly, the monster vomits out another burst; so close that the noise deafens me. I bury my face in my arms. Fortunately almost every one of the projectiles comes down outside the crater. And now all at once I realize that it is I who am here— *alive* in this crater, surrounded by scorching walls, face to face with the very mouth of the fire. Why have I got myself in this trap, alone and without the slightest chance of help? Nobody in the world has any suspicion of the strange adventure on which I have embarked, and nobody, for that matter, could now do the slightest thing about it. Better not think about it. . . .

Without a break the grim, steady growling continues to rise from the depths of that throat, only outroared at intervals by the bellowing and belching of lava. It's too much; I can feel myself giving up. I turn my back on it, and try, on all fours, to scramble up the slope, which has now become incredibly steep and crumbles and gives way under my weight, which is dragging me down, down. . . . "Steady, now," I say to myself. "Keep calm for a moment. Let's work it out. Let's work it out properly. Or else, my boy, this is the end of *you.*"

Little by little, by immense exertions, I regain control of my movements, as well as the mental steadiness I need. I persuade myself to climb *calmly* up this short slope, which keeps crumbling away under my feet. When I reach the top, I stand upright for just a moment. Then, crossing the two glowing fissures that still intersect my course, I reach the part of the rim from where there is a way down to the world of ordinary peaceful things.

THE STORY OF MAURICE WILSON

DENNIS ROBERTS

A MYSTIC ON MT. EVEREST
ERIC SHIPTON

*About three hundred yards above Camp III we found the
body of Maurice Wilson, who had attempted to climb Mount
Everest alone the previous year and about whom nothing more
had been heard. From a diary which we found on his body and
from subsequent enquiries we were able to piece together his
curious story. He was a man of about thirty-seven and had
served in France during the last war. He had developed a theory
that if a man were to go without food for three weeks he would
reach a stage of semi-consciousness on the borderland of life
and death, when his physical mind would establish direct communication with his soul. When he emerged from this state he
would be cleansed of all bodily and spiritual ills; he would be
as a new-born child but with the benefit of the experience of his
previous life, and with greatly increased physical and spiritual
strength. Wilson had fanatical faith in his theory. He believed
moreover that he had seen a vision in which he had received
divine instruction to preach the doctrine to mankind. Somehow*

the word "Everest" had featured in the vision, and he thought that it was intended to indicate the means by which he could achieve his purpose. Obviously if he succeeded in reaching the summit of Mount Everest single-handed, the feat would cause no small stir, and his theory would receive wide publicity.

He knew nothing whatever about mountaineering. At the time, however, the Houston-Everest Flight was receiving considerable press publicity. Presumably this gave him the idea that if he were to fly a plane as high as he could and crash it on the side of the mountain he would be able to climb the rest of the way to the summit and return on foot. So with this object in view he learned to fly, bought a small aeroplane and set out for India. At Cairo he was stopped and turned back by the authorities. But eventually he reached Purnea in India where his machine was confiscated. He went to Darjeeling where he stayed for four months, training himself and making secret preparations for his journey to Mount Everest. He got in touch with some of the Sherpas who had been with us the year before and they agreed to smuggle him through Sikkim and into Tibet. He then covered up his tracks by paying for his room at the hotel six months in advance so that he could keep it locked with his things inside, and gave it out that he had been invited by a friend to go on a tiger shoot. It was some time before the authorities discovered that he was missing.

In the meantime, by wearing a disguise and travelling at night he had succeeded in passing through Sikkim and into Tibet. There he travelled more openly, but with practically no baggage and by avoiding the big places he and his three Sherpa companions attracted no attention. When they arrived at Rongbuk he told the abbot of the monastery that he was a member of the 1933 expedition and induced him to hand over a few small items of equipment that we had left there. He had evidently made a good impression upon the old man, who when we visited the monastery in 1935 talked to us a great deal about him. He left the Sherpas at Rongbuk and started up the glacier alone with the complete conviction that he would reach the summit in three or four days. He had with him a small shaving mirror with which he proposed to heliograph to those at Rongbuk from the summit, so as to provide proof that he had actually reached it. He was used to starving himself and intended to live on a small quantity of rice water. It was early in April and he encountered the usual spring gales on the East Rongbuk glacier. He appears to have reached a point somewhere about Camp II before he was forced to retreat, exhausted.

After a fortnight's rest he set out again, this time with the Sherpas. They reached Camp III and the Sherpas showed him a dump of food which we had left about half a mile beyond, and which contained all kinds of luxuries such as chocolate, Ovaltine, sardines, baked beans and biscuits, with which he was delighted. He left the Sherpas at Camp III and went on alone. He had evidently expected to find intact the steps which we had cut in the slopes below the North Col, and he was bitterly disappointed to find nothing but bare wind-swept ice and snow. Though he had an ice-axe, he did not know how to use it and could make little headway up the slopes. He camped alone on the rocks near the dump and set out day after day to renew his fruitless attempts to reach the Col. Though he had plenty of food, he was gradually weakened by the severe conditions. This was clear from the entries in his diary, which became shorter and less coherent towards the end. But he would not give up and still clung to his faith in divine inspiration. The last entry was on the 31st of May, 1934. He died in his sleep, lying in his small tent. This had been smashed by storms, and all the fragments, except the guy-lines which were attached to boulders, had been swept away.

The Sherpas said they had waited a month for him at Camp III. This is clearly untrue for they would certainly have visited

the food-dump from time to time and would have found the
body. We had two of the men with us in 1935, but one had been
attached to Spender's party and the other had been sent down
to fetch some stuff from Camp II on the day that we found the
body. We buried it in a crevasse.

From *Upon That Mountain*

PROLOGUE
NORTH COL: MAY, 1934

A plume of powder snow was streaming from the northern
face of Everest. The cold at 21,000 feet was numbing and the
wind tore with insensate fury round the solitary tent that was
pitched a little below the North Col. Inside the tent three men
were arguing; two were Sherpas, the third was an obstinate
Yorkshireman who still believed that he could climb alone the
remaining 8,000 feet to the summit of the highest mountain in
the world.

They argued far into the night, having to shout to make
themselves heard above the splitting roar of the wind. The
Sherpas, born and bred in the high hills of the Himalaya, knew
that the summit of Everest was beyond the reach of any of
them. But the Yorkshireman was fiercely determined to go on;
if he had doubts about the outcome of his lone assault he hid
them behind an air of confident bravado.

"Wait here for ten days," he said at last to the Sherpas. "Then
if I don't come back, return by yourselves."

And very early the next morning he set out to finish his
solitary battle with Everest, carrying with him three loaves of
bread, two tins of oatmeal and a small Union Jack.

The Sherpas knew that they would never see him again. But
day after day, with the weather rapidly worsening, they clung

to their precarious foothold at the approaches to North Col. Only when the monsoon broke, over a week later, did they return sadly to the Rongbuk Monastery; and from there news seeped out to the world that Captain Maurice Wilson, M.C. was dead.

So ended the most incredible story in all the eventful history of Mount Everest; a story compounded in almost equal parts of tragedy and heroism.

It was his attempt to prove a fantastic theory that led Maurice Wilson to make his lone quixotic challenge. He was past his physical prime when he first set foot on Everest; he had an injured arm, he had no mountaineering experience, yet he tried to climb the highest mountain in the world alone. And, after overcoming the most incredible obstacles, he reached a height of some 22,000 feet. There his quest ended in a wilderness of ice and snow and tearing wind that wore out his body but never damped the flame of his spirit.

The fact that Maurice Wilson was not the first man to reach the summit of Everest is of no more consequence than the fact that Scott was not the first man to reach the South Pole. It was the manner of their failing that has won for both men a claim to immortality.

The South Pole, the summit of Everest; how much more did these two objectives symbolize to those who sought them than mere pinpoints on the earth's surface where no man had ever stood before?

Maurice Wilson's executors have now for the first time made available his diaries and letters. For this we must thank them; for without their co-operation the memory of one of the most remarkable figures of our age could not have been perpetuated.

THE MAN

Maurice Wilson was born in Bradford, on April 21st, 1898. He was the third of four sons born to Mark and Sarah Wilson, and his childhood was happy, with a humdrum, unexciting sort of happiness. His father was employed at the time of his birth as a weaver's overlooker in one of the largest Bradford Mills—a responsible and well-paid position—and from his earliest years Maurice enjoyed the comfort and security of a solid middle-class home and upbringing. In later years, the Wilson family could, had they so wished, have exchanged this comfort for some degree of luxury. For Mark Wilson was a hard-working and able man, who at quite an early age became one of the directors of the Holme Topp Mill in Little Horton. But he gave much of his money away to deserving local causes and soon in the area around Bradford the Wilson family became widely known and deeply respected for their charitable works.

Maurice inherited his father's business ability and also something even more precious—his sympathy and understanding for those whose lives were less favored by fortune than his own. Bradford, in the early years of the century, was the scene of a good deal of poverty. Mark Wilson had no wish for his young son to hide his eyes from the unhappier side of life, and the result was that Maurice conceived in the Bradford slums a depth of feeling for the world's lame ducks and underdogs that he was never to lose.

He was educated at the Carlton Road Secondary School, and soon proved himself a bright but not exceptional pupil. Physically he was strong, and the photos of him as a child depict him as a stocky, thick-set little boy with an independent air. . . .

We pick up Maurice Wilson years later. The ex-soldier of World War One has taught himself to fly. His plane is called Ever Wrest. *He is at Camp III with his Sherpa companions. From his diary, we read the following entries:*

"*May 17th. Thurs.* It's snowing like the devil, and I can see less than 200 feet. Had bit of a head, but shall start tomorrow if weather O.K. Have decided not to take short cut to Camp V as at first intended as should have to cut my own steps up the ice-fall; that's silly when there should already be handrope and steps leading to old Camp IV. [It seems that Wilson seriously expected the steps cut by Ruttledge over a year ago to be still intact.] Not much to do except eat and sleep. What do you think I had yesterday? Anchovy paste from Fortnum and Masons! Usually we feed twice a day. First about 6.30 when Rintsi comes along with smoked tea or Ovaltine, followed half an hour later by soup with meat in it. Then at 2 P.M. up comes the same again. Everything tastes horribly of smoke. . . !

"*May 18th. Fri.* Nothing to do all day. . . . It's still snowing and blowing like the D. Went to see how the boys were getting on at 3 P.M., but was soon glad to get back to sleeping bag. Rintsi went to store dump and got some fine Ever-Ready batteries— a darned sight better than those we bought in Darjeeling. He also bagged a 20 ft. bamboo mast for firewood; doesn't go to the bother of breaking it up, but has the thing propped its whole length across fire and pulls in the slack as it burns away. . . . Just going to have a bit of shut eye.

"*May 19th. Sat.* Another couple of days and it will be 12 months since I said cheerio to you all. How time flies. Weather still too windy and far too much drift snow to start off today, so am just sitting or rather lying quiet. Feeling bit better after long lay up out of sun.

"*May 20th. Sun.* Snow stopped and sun out but wind still v. bad. These violet rays are terrible. Have thick blanket strapped over tent, but can still feel them through my balaclava helmet. When I've had my Irish Stew shall have to get out yet another helmet.

"*May 21st. Mon.* Had enough bed the last few days for a year. Terrible when you can't put your head down for aching nerves. Weather better. We start again tomorrow."

And the next day, almost a year after he had left England,

Wilson started on the penultimate stage of his lone assault. He had slept badly on the night of the 21st and woke feeling cold; he found himself shivering as he waited for Rinzing to brew up the tea, and took twenty minutes to lace up his climbing boots. He breakfasted as the pale light of dawn came flooding coldly over the rim of North Col. Then he looked outside the tent and saw the crest of Everest, snow-plumed and deceptively near. The wind had dropped, and as the sun came streaming over the eastern peaks he began to climb, very slowly, towards the ice fall.

Rinzing had promised to come with him until it was noon to show him the approximate route used by Ruttledge; and to start with the two men made reasonable progress up the lower slopes. But soon the gradient steepened, the ice became broken into monstrous blocks and seracs, and the newly-fallen snow masked the host of minor crevasses that split the face of the ice in all directions. Wilson looked about in vain for traces of the track hewn out by Ruttledge; the steps had been destroyed and the rope guides swept away. An hour after breaking camp they began to cut steps.

Wilson was so inexpert at this that he had to ask Rinzing to lead, and he watched the Sherpa carefully to see how the steps were made. After twenty minutes he took over the lead, but soon found that the additional effort to step cutting quickly sapped his energy—probably his lack of skill meant that his exertions were far greater than those of an experienced mountaineer. Soon they came to an especially steep slope, of some sixty degrees, crowned by a number of unstable-looking seracs. Their progress was reduced to a panting crawl.

It took them a couple of hours to cut steps up the forty feet of slope; but at last they emerged onto a narrow ledge among the grotesque seracs and pinnacles. At one end of the ledge a steep little couloir led upwards towards the great crevasse.

It was after noon and Rinzing told Wilson he could come no further, as darkness would fall before he could make the descent to Camp III. They shook hands and the Sherpa began to retrace his steps. Soon he had vanished from sight, and Wilson felt very much alone.

He worked his way among the seracs to the foot of the little couloir; it looked, from close to, even steeper than he had feared. It was two o'clock now, and realizing he could hardly climb it that night, Wilson decided to pitch camp. It was difficult to find a spot level enough to set up his tent, and he was tempted to make use of the open space at the foot of the couloir. There, however, the ground had been worn smooth by the passage of countless small avalanches, which periodically came sweeping down the couloir and then, after some fifty feet, cascaded over the steepening cliff. He decided—wisely—to prefer the discomfort of the seracs to the danger of the avalanches, and eventually managed to wedge his tent, at a somewhat alarming angle, between two reasonably stable pinnacles.

He was exhausted; and now he was alone he began once again to neglect his health. He could not be bothered to prepare a proper meal, but ate only some chocolate and dry biscuits before crawling into his sleeping-bag. He wanted desperately to sleep, but sleep did not come easily. Surely that night he must have been haunted by the spectre of impending failure; he had planned to reach the Col by nightfall, but he was only some third of the way there. And tomorrow he would be alone.

May 23rd dawned mercifully fine. He was up early and cooked himself a good breakfast of hot stew; but he was surprised to find how long everything took. He had woken at six; it was seven-thirty before he had cooked breakfast, and after nine before he had struck camp. The sun's rays were surprisingly warm on his back as a little before ten o'clock he stood looking up at the couloir. Wilson hoped that the milder weather did not herald the approach of the monsoon. From higher up on the shoulder of Everest he could hear the distant roar of avalanches, and he dreaded being caught by one in the couloir. He knew it was near here that in 1922 seven porters had been killed by avalanching snow. He began, slowly, laboriously and inexpertly, cutting steps up the edge of the couloir, avoiding the center which he saw was liable to avalanche. And as morning passed into afternoon he must have realized the hopelessness of his task.

For his headway was pitiably slow and cost him great effort. Every few minutes he had to stop and gasp for breath. Once his foothold gave way, and he slid back for twenty feet, starting a small avalanche, which, as he watched it, gained in bulk and momentum and went cascading down the ice fall until, far below, it shot down and outward onto the East Rongbuk Glacier.

It took him three hours to climb the couloir. Then, still cutting steps, he traversed the slope that led up sharply toward the great crevasse. He pitched camp in a poor position on a shelf, tilted at twenty degrees, in the middle of the wind-swept slope. A blizzard would have blown him straight onto the glacier, now nearly a thousand feet below. But he was lucky. The night was calm, though terribly cold. At 4 P.M., too exhausted to prepare a meal, he fell into his sleeping-bag. "Just," he wrote, "going to have a few minutes shut-eye." When he woke it was dawn and he was bitterly cold.

There had in the night been fifty-seven degrees of frost and Wilson feared he must surely have frost-bite. But after a couple of hours he found he could move both fingers and toes, and it was clear that he had somehow escaped it. He had, however, a headache, and a throat which two cups of luke-warm tea did little to alleviate. He ate a small quantity of snow, and then at 9 A.M. started off again.

His first obstacle was the crevasse.

He approached it cautiously, which was just as well, for it proved to have an unstable lower lip and looked quite bottomless. It averaged some thirty feet in width, and its walls were sheer, pale blue at the top, merging into royal blue, deep blue and indigo as it plummeted into unseen depths. Wilson worked his way along it, keeping to the left where the crevasse seemed to narrow slightly. After about an hour he came to an unstable-looking snow bridge.

Snow bridges present a tricky problem even to the experienced mountaineer; there is no certain way of gauging their strength. Wilson tried for a couple of hours to find an alternative route over the crevasse. There was none. He sat down and ate his lunch—five dry biscuits. Then, because postponement of the issue was obviously no solution to it, he knelt down and prayed and when he had finished he got up and walked across the bridge as carefully as he could. And the bridge held.

When he reached the other side he found a not too difficult slope, which he traversed with the cutting of only a few steps for some hundred and fifty yards. Then, at about noon, he reached the foot of the last ice cliff, guarding the comparatively easy slopes to the North Col. Another two hundred feet and he would reach the Col. He looked in vain for some crack in the apparently unscalable face: sixty feet of ice and rock, not only vertical but actually in some places overhanging. He remembered the chimney he had seen from Camp III, but in his preoccupation with crossing the crevasse, he realized he had worked away from it. He started to hack his way along the foot of the cliff apparently oblivious of the danger of avalanches, and at last, more by luck than judgment, found himself working toward the chimney.

That night when he pitched camp at its foot, he was at a height of only a little under 23,000 feet. Once again he was too exhausted to cook a meal. Nor did he choose a good site for his tent—it would in all probability have been impossible to find a "good" site on the ice fall, but Wilson was too weary to find even a passable one. He set up his tent at an angle of thirty-five degrees and scooped and hacked away the snow and ice to prevent his rolling down the icefall in his sleep.

He spent a miserable night.

The dawn of May 24th saw him crawl very slowly out of his

tent and prepare his breakfast, "took 2 hours for damned water to boil." He used his matches as an improvised candlestand, and they soon became useless—saturated with grease. Wilson realized he now had no means of making either heat or light. But he refused to give up.

For seven hours he tried to climb the chimney.

How far up he got we shall never know—probably not very far. But the fact that he failed to climb it is not really important; what matters is that he went on trying. The odds are that an experienced mountaineer could probably have climbed the chimney in about an hour—though even this is by no means certain as it may not have been on the exact route used by Ruttledge, or if it was, its composition may have altered. In any case it was, for Wilson, an insurmountable obstacle: every difficulty he had so far met with he had overcome. But here was a barrier that courage and determination alone could never break. By the end of May 24th, when he stumbled into his tent, still at the foot of the chimney, he must have known with terrible certainty that he would never climb Mount Everest alone.

The next day, having neither drunk nor eaten anything hot for over twenty-four hours, he set out again. But he was too weak to climb more than a few yards above his tent.

He realized that he was now faced with the same three courses as on the East Rongbuk Glacier a month before. He could climb up the chimney until he fell to his death; he could stay in his tent and wait for death to come to him; or he could go back, and try to persuade the Sherpas to accompany him still higher.

Wilson had still sufficient sanity to realize that only the last course afforded him the slightest hope of reaching the top of Everest. It seems from his diary—which from now on becomes slightly incoherent and extremely difficult to read—that he hoped to return to Camp III, rest there for a couple of days and then persuade Rinzing to carry supplies for him up to Camp IV; he evidently had sufficient faith in the Sherpa's mountaineering skill to believe that the two of them could between them climb the chimney onto the slopes of North Col. . . .

And so at about ten o'clock Wilson began his second flight from Everest; a flight even more incredible than the first.

In less than five hours, weak and unskilled as he was, he slipped and slithered his way down fifteen hundred feet of extremely difficult ice. Twice he fell badly, and rolled over and over until the soft snow checked him. Each time he struggled quickly to his feet, rubbing the pain from his ribs; they might for all he knew have been broken; he had no time to find out; he only knew that somehow he must reach Camp III before nightfall. He came to the crevasse, and the snow bridge looked even frailer than before; but once again it held. He found his steps down the couloir, and half scrambled, half fell down them. In the twilight haze he could pick out far below him, the tents of Camp III. He saw the Sherpas stumbling upward to meet him, and almost sobbing with relief he fell into Rinzing's arms and was carried into his tent. A bowl of hot soup and then, quite literally half-dead with exhaustion, he fell asleep. And he slept for thirty hours.

He woke at 11 P.M. on Saturday, May 26th, and his Sherpas had a hot meal ready and waiting. Their kindness and their obvious anxiety touched Wilson deeply; but when they spoke of returning to Rongbuk he simply shook his head.

"I didn't come back," he said, "because I'd given up—I came back because I want you to come with me to Camp IV."

"IF I DON'T COME BACK . . ."

Up to now Wilson's battered little diary has provided a fairly complete account of his day-by-day progress on to the upper slopes of Everest. But for the last days of his life the diary entries are short and pitiably incoherent; thus of his third attempt to climb the mountain we can gain only a blurred fragmentary picture.

We know that on Saturday and Sunday he remained resting in his tent. His diary simply reads:

"26th *Sat.* Stayed in bed.

27th *Sun.* " " "

and we can imagine him, most of the time asleep, curled up in his bag, while the Sherpas in their tent a few yards away cooked food and probably reflected on the hopelessness of their position; and the wind tore and thundered around them incessantly, and the cold and the inhuman desolation sapped away the very desire to live.

It must by now have been obvious to Wilson that if he went on alone, it could only be to his death; and he must therefore have used all his eloquence to try to persuade the Sherpas to accompany him at least to the top of the ice fall. And by the night of Sunday 27th, he apparently believed that his eloquence had taken effect; for he wrote next morning in his diary: "28*th Mon.* Tewang wanted to go back, but persuaded them go with me to Camp V. This will be last effort, and I feel successful. . . ."

But in actual fact either he had misunderstood the Sherpas or else his mind had begun to wander—it is quite common for those who stay too long at high altitudes to suffer from delusions —for Tewang and Rinzing soon made it abundantly plain that under no circumstances would they go a step further.

Tewang indeed was in no shape to continue, it would be as much as he could manage safely to decend, let alone ascend, the mountain; and Rinzing, who had climbed to over 27,000 feet on the previous expedition, knew enough about the upper slopes of Everest to realize that even if they climbed the ice fall the summit would still be utterly beyond them. Both the Sherpas, men born and bred in the high hills of the Himalaya, men whose judgment was far more balanced than that of Wilson, said emphatically that it was impossible to push on further. It was too late, they said; in a few days the monsoon would break; they pointed out that they were all too weak (Wilson was partially snow-blinded and suffering from exhaustion and lack of oxygen); they had not enough porters, they said, or enough climbing equipment to force a way up the ice fall and establish on the Col a well-stocked camp; and, last but by no means least, they knew that Wilson lacked the technical mountaineering skill to lead the ascent safely. With every justification, the Sherpas pleaded with him to abandon his attempt. With every justification, they refused to climb even another fifty feet.

And some time during that afternoon of Monday, May 28th, it must have become plain to Wilson that Tewang and Rinzing would indeed come with him no further.

"Faith," he had once written, "is not faith that wavers when its prayers remain unanswered." Did he still, he must now have asked himself, hold fast to his original belief? Now that it seemed as though God had deserted him, now that all his theories seemed about to be disproved, did he still believe that he could climb Mount Everest alone?

His was the sort of faith that remains inviolate in the face of all adversity, and he began that night to make preparations for his last attempt.

He rummaged about among his kit until he found the "flag of friendship"—the silk pennant on which his closest friends had signed their names before he left London. He decided to take it with him. He also put into his rucksack the oxygen equipment and the bare minimum of supplies; he knew he would have to travel light, and he took with him food for only seven days; he reckoned if all went well he could climb the mountain in four or five days, and the exhilaration of success would sustain him on his descent.

He had a hot meal that Sunday night at a little before six-thirty; then as he struggled into his sleeping bag, there came over him the strangest feeling; he became convinced that someone was by his side. The only sound was the tearing roar of the wind. The two Sherpas lay resting in their tent. Yet still Wilson felt that he was not alone. "Strange," he wrote, "but I feel that there is somebody with me in tent all the time."

And before this feeling is attributed to an unbalanced state of mind, it should perhaps be remembered that Frank Smythe had undergone a similar experience on the upper slopes of Everest the year before, an experience that he writes about very vividly. "All the time," he tells us, "that I was climbing alone, I had the feeling that there was someone with me. I felt that were I to slip I should be held up and supported as though I had a companion with me with a rope. Sir Ernest Shackleton had the same experience when crossing the mountains of South Georgia after his hazardous open-boat journey from Elephant Island, and he narrates how he and his companion felt that there was an extra "someone" in the party. "When I reached the ledge I felt I ought to eat something to keep up my strength. All I had brought with me was a slab of Kendal Mint Cake. This I took out of my pocket and, carefully dividing it into two halves, turned round with one half in my hand to offer my companion. . . ."

That night Wilson slept reasonably well, and the next morning—Tuesday, May 29th—he was up early and as soon as it was light he went across to the Sherpas' tent.

It was chillingly cold and a long banner of snow streamed from the summit of Everest. The wind was very strong, and after covering even the few paces to the porters' tent, Wilson found himself gasping for breath. He came straight to the point. He told them he was determined to make a last attempt. Would they, he asked, come with him? Again Tewang and Rinzing refused; under no circumstances, they said, would they climb another step.

There was, in later years, some talk of the Sherpas having deserted Wilson; but both the word and also its implication of disloyalty are quite out of place. For only if they had made with their leader a joint suicide pact could the Sherpas have been reasonably expected to throw away their lives by joining in so foredoomed a venture.

It was a sad little drama that was, early that morning, played out to its inevitable climax in the porters' tent. The more Tewang and Rinzing pleaded with Wilson to return, the more obstinate he became. When at last he realized he would never get them to change their minds, he must have known in his heart what the end of his quest would be; but he ended the argument by saying simply:

"Wait here for ten days. Then if I don't come back, return by yourselves."

He went out, packed up his tent, his sleeping-bag and his few pieces of equipment. Then, alone and very slowly, he began to climb up the ice fall towards the slopes of the North Col.

He did not get very far.

Just how much he suffered in those last days is something that will never be known; and this perhaps is as it should be, for the Calvary of a brave man is something strictly personal between that man and his God. But the half-dozen lines in his diary and the reports of the Sherpas when they returned later to Kalimpong give the bare facts.

It was in the latter half of July that the first rumors of Wilson's death began to filter through to the outside world. His three Sherpas had returned to Kalimpong; here they were interviewed, interrogated and cross-examined for week after week, and though their story contained a number of inconsistencies, it did, at least, seem to establish the certainty of Wilson's death.

So on July 20th papers all over the world blazoned out their headlines—"Lone Death on Everest," "Pluck or Suicide," "Excelsior with a Union Jack." The publicity would have pleased Wilson, though he would have noticed a little sadly that no mention was ever made of the motive behind his solitary challenge. "What?" is always an easier question to answer than "Why?"

When the evidence of the Sherpas had been correlated, filtered and checked, the gist of it did not amount to much; indeed all they had to say could be, and was, condensed into three short articles printed on July 20th by three London newspapers. The *Daily Telegraph* said:

DRAMA OF
LONE EVEREST
CLIMBER

Left his Porters
behind

Diet of Bread and
Porridge

FEAR THAT HE HAS
PERISHED
BEYOND CAMP III ON
THE RUTTLEDGE PATH

It is feared that Mr. Maurice Wilson, the young British airman who was making a gallant attempt to climb Mount Everest alone, has lost his life.

News received here (Darjeeling) today states that his effort to conquer the world's highest peak has ended in tragedy. The porters who accompanied this "Do-or-Die" Briton relate a dramatic story of how, at a height of over 21,000 feet, he went on alone, carrying only a light tent, three loaves of bread, two tins of porridge and a camera. . . .

Two porters accompanied him as far as the site of the Camp III—21,000 feet—established by the Ruttledge Expedition. They then deemed it impossible to make farther progress up Mount Everest without ropes and more men to hew the track. But Mr. Wilson, according to the porters, there and then decided to go on alone. . . .

After Camp III the track lies over a glacier on which avalanches are constantly crashing down, and there are also treacherous crevasses. The temperature there must have exceeded fifty degrees of frost.

Mountaineers regard this region as one where only experienced, roped parties have a reasonable prospect of getting through.

So ends the story of Maurice Wilson. At the time of his death there were few to mourn for him; for he was, to those who read of his exploits, an object more of pity than of admiration. It was as though Longfellow had already provided him with an epitaph:

> There in the twilight cold and grey,
> Lifeless, but beautiful, he lay,
> And from the sky, serene and far,
> A voice fell, like a falling star,
>   Excelsior!

Nor in the years that followed was much attention paid to his lone quixotic challenge. Of the many hundred thousand words written about Everest and the men who tried to climb her, only a few hundred were devoted to Maurice Wilson.

Yet did he really die in vain? Must he be remembered only as a pitiable failure? Should we not rather recall the words of George Leigh-Mallory as he stood at the summit of a great Himalaya peak: "Have we vanquished an enemy?" he asked himself. And the answer was, "None but ourselves. . . . Have we gained success? The word means nothing here." It is true that if we judge him by results, or by his technical skill, Wilson was no great mountaineer. He never in all his life climbed a single worth-while peak. But his spirit was that of Mallory. He failed to conquer Everest; but he never failed himself, or mankind, or his ideal. He possessed, in spite of all his faults—his recklessness and foolish pride—the spirit that makes men great.

No four words could tell more clearly a man's character than those pencilled, very faintly, as the last entry of Maurice Wilson's diary: "Off again, gorgeous day."

about the author

Harry Roskolenko, born in New York, ran off to sea at the age of thirteen. He was a Second Officer in the merchant marine during World War II and is the author of many books dealing with the South Pacific, Australia, New Guinea, Indo China—where he was a correspondent in 1947. He has made two solo trips. One took him around the world on a scooter, and the second—all of the Nile.